SERENITY

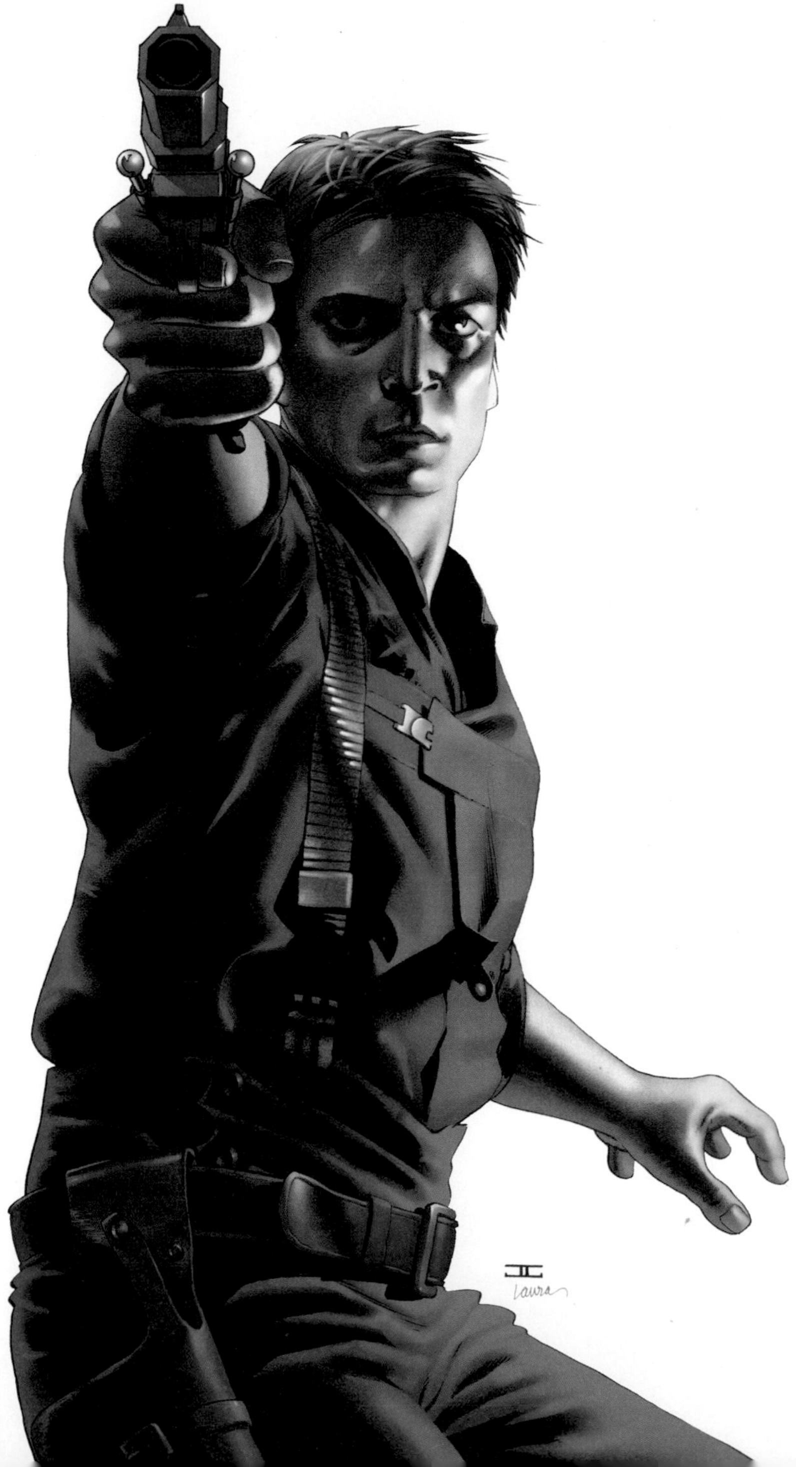

Art by John Cassaday
Colors by Laura Martin

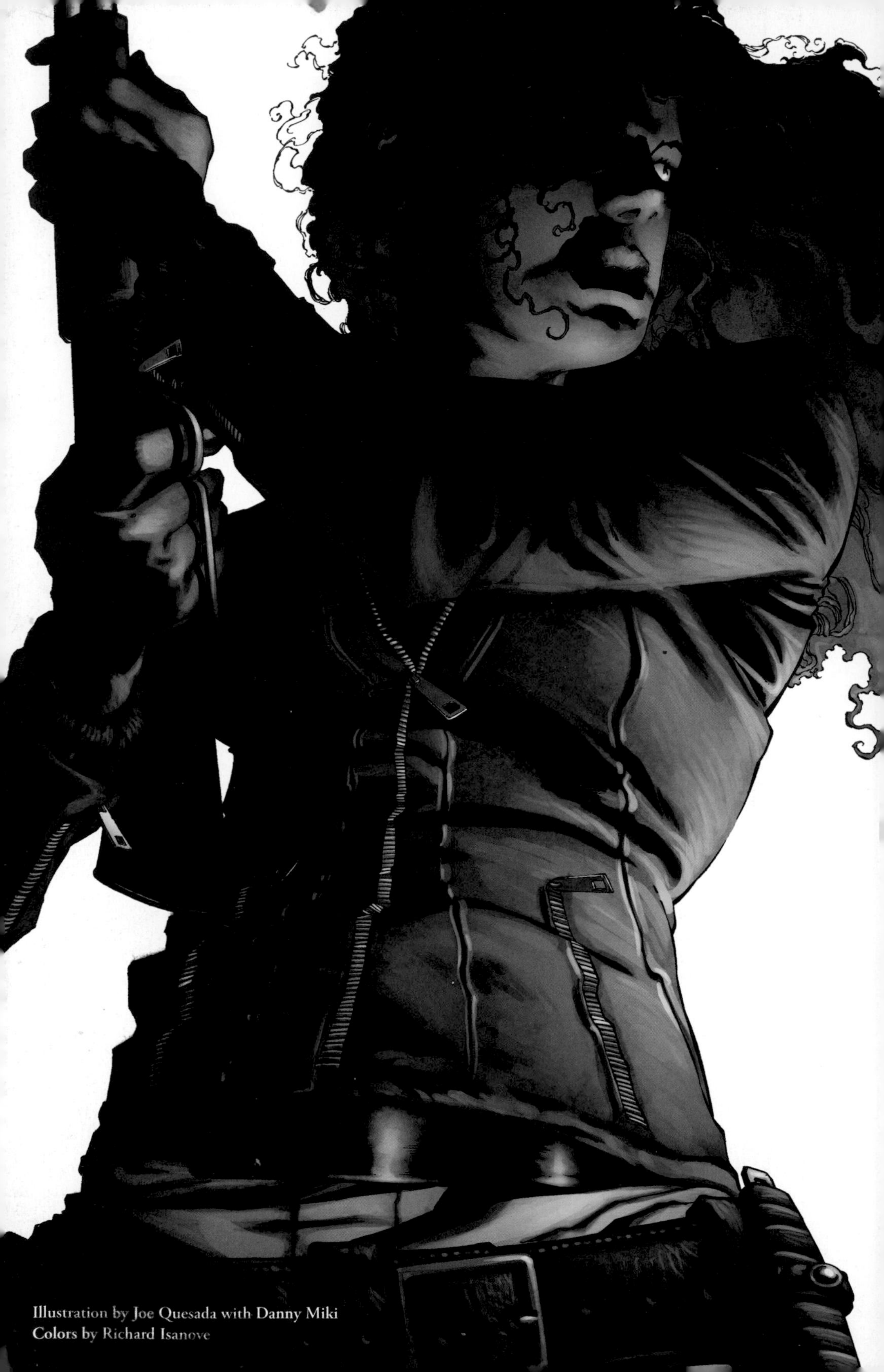

Illustration by Joe Quesada with Danny Miki
Colors by Richard Isanove

SERENITY

THOSE LEFT BEHIND

STORY BY

JOSS WHEDON & BRETT MATTHEWS

SCRIPT BY

BRETT MATTHEWS

ART BY

WILL CONRAD

COLORS BY

LAURA MARTIN

LETTERS BY

MICHAEL HEISLER

FRONT COVER ART BY

ADAM HUGHES

BACK COVER ART BY

SEAN PHILLIPS

DARK HORSE BOOKS™

PUBLISHER
MIKE RICHARDSON

EDITOR
SCOTT ALLIE

ASSISTANT EDITORS
MATT DRYER & DAVE MARSHALL

COLLECTION DESIGNER
HEIDI FAINZA

ART DIRECTOR
LIA RIBACCHI

Special thanks to Cindy Chang and Veronika Beltran at Universal Studios.
Special thanks also to Michael Boretz, J. P. Bernardo, Debbie Olshan, & Deborah Hsu.

帶勁

Published by
Dark Horse Books
A division of
Dark Horse Comics, Inc.
10956 SE Main Street
Milwaukie OR 97222

darkhorse.com

To find a comics shop in your area,
call the Comic Shop Locator Service toll-free at 1-888-266-4226

First edition: January 2006
ISBN: 1-59307-449-2

3 5 7 9 10 8 6 4

Printed in U.S.A.

This volume collects issues one through three of the Dark Horse comic-book series *Serenity: Those Left Behind.*

帶 INTRODUCTION 勁

When I was very young, before I could read, I remember being interested in comic books. Our bedtime was not negotiable, but we could delay "lights out" for another half hour if we read anything. I mostly looked at the pictures; I could make out "a" and "the," and then simply tried to piece together a story. I could tell that Jughead liked to eat, Archie was broke, Betty was nice, and Veronica was mean. There are only so many times you can read the same ones, though, so my dad would take my brother and me to Whyte Avenue. Not too far down from Uncle Albert's Pancake House (burned down since then) was the Wee Book Inn, a store that had an odor a bit like someone's grandmother's house. Not mine, but someone's. I remember the dirty orange carpet, frayed and ragged. The wooden shelves were tall and packed with worn covers of books read many times over. Pages were yellowed and paperbacks had arched spines like old sway-backed horses. It was an old folks' home for secondhand books, with that smell of old newsprint and slightly musty wood. There were stacks of magazines with fat, contented cats sleeping on them that you could pet without fear of being scratched. If ever there was a mystical "Ye Olde Magic Shoppe" in my life, this was it. It was a trading post for old books, and more importantly, comics. My dad would have us bring all the comics we could bear to part with, and we would watch as the clerk would shuffle through them, calculating their value. I felt as though I was in the days of the Klondike, come down from my claim in the hills and waiting for the assayer to separate the fool's gold from the real thing. His appraisal would determine how many secondhand comics we could walk away with. Always fewer than what we came in with, but my Pops would pull out his wallet, careful to make sure we never left with a smaller stack. Comics were our treasure, our booty, and we would rush up to our rooms and file them away carefully on our very own spinning comic rack.

Soon, Archie, Dot, and Richie Rich gave way to Spider-Man, Captain America, X-Men, and Alpha Flight (Canada's very own super team). Now, around this time, my memories blur a bit, but what I remember is this—I wanted to be a superhero. My brain was constantly calculating my super moves, my super costume, what powers I would have, how I would use them, and with whom I would share my incredible secret. My brother was in, my parents were out—lest they force me to use my newfound abilities on chores. There were, however, no radioactive spiders available to me, no toxic waste sites, and I found out very quickly, despite my brother's urging, that jumping off the garage roof with two kites to sweep over the neighborhood didn't work. When the price of comics increased, so did my interest in girls and cars, and my treasure was relegated to the darkness of the crawlspace of our house, carefully packed in plastic bags and taped twice, not once. My desire to be a superhero, however, never abated. I couldn't help but think about how being able to fly and being bulletproof would help me in any endeavor I chose.

And then there was Joss. I met him in a small, dimly lit office, where he regaled me with tales of adventure, swashbuckling, shooting, spaceships, and narrow escapes. Um, where do I sign? He gave me a new identity, a costume, a gun, and a long brown duster for a cape. I remember that meeting so well; it was like a superhero "origin" issue. I remember Joss looking at Polaroid photos of my first costume fitting, holding up the one with the duster and gun saying, "Action figure, anyone?"

Never in my wildest. Like some sort of super-team benefactor, Joss made superheroes out of all of us, complete with a super-hideout spaceship. During filming, we'd all retreat to our dressing room trailers and emerge like Supermen with our alter egos. The boots, the suspenders, gun holstered low on my hip . . . with a flick and a spin of that wicked awesome coat over my shoulders, I became someone else.

So, I guess the message I want to leave you with is this: What you hold in your hand is not just a comic. It is much more. It is a handbook. It is a guide. It is reference material for when you become a superhero. I have found the secret, you see. To become a superhero, all you have to do is want it badly enough, and comics are the fuel to that fire.

Incidentally, you hold in your hand my favorite (*favourite* for Canadians) . . . comic . . . ever. Dark Horse and our cover artists have given us a great introduction to Joss' world of comic action heroes. They amazed us from the first issue, packed with shooting, crashing, punching, and splatting. Thank you, everyone. I'll be placing this series in my comic book rack, just as soon as I get this home. It will be wrapped and double-taped.

—NATHAN FILLION

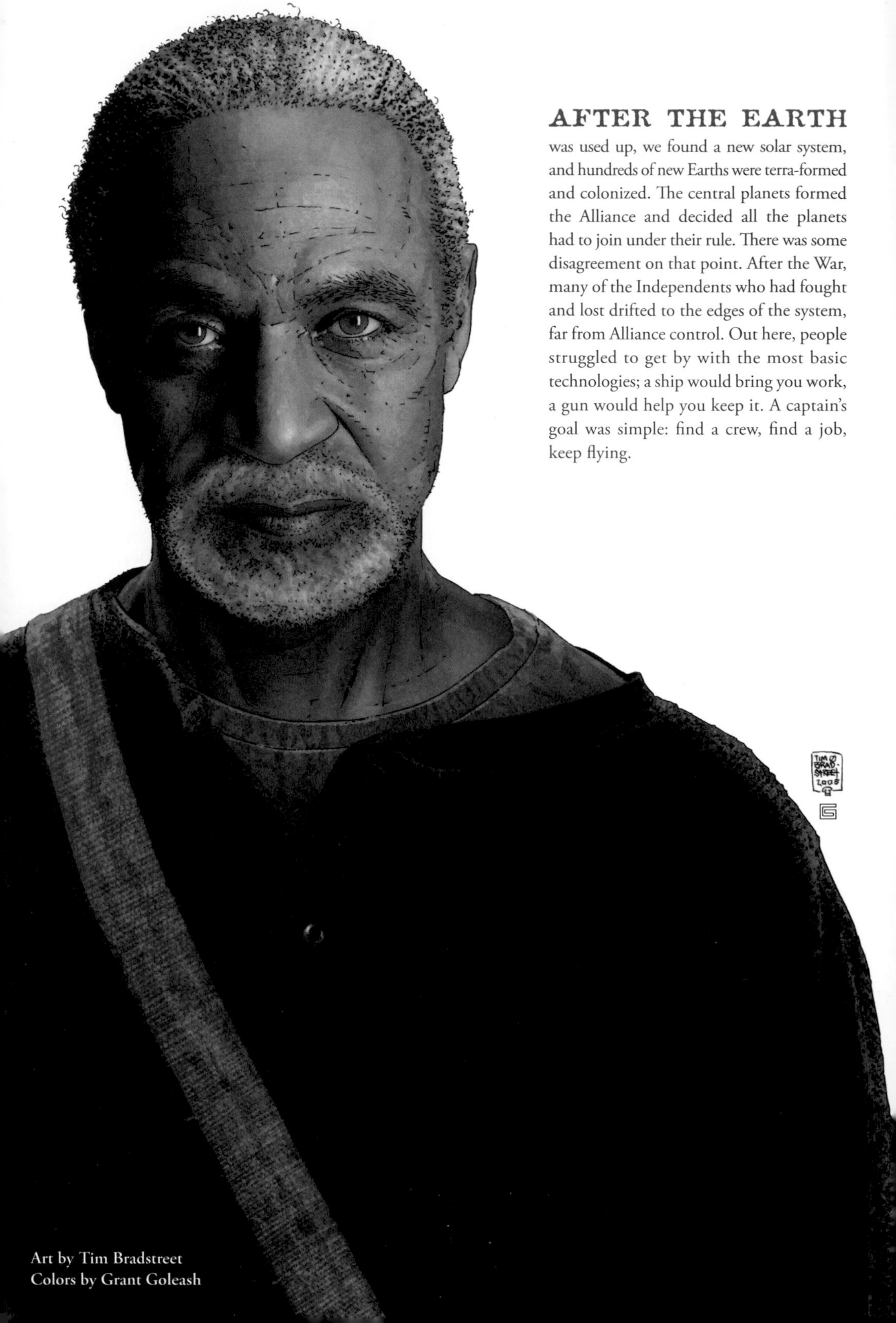

AFTER THE EARTH

was used up, we found a new solar system, and hundreds of new Earths were terra-formed and colonized. The central planets formed the Alliance and decided all the planets had to join under their rule. There was some disagreement on that point. After the War, many of the Independents who had fought and lost drifted to the edges of the system, far from Alliance control. Out here, people struggled to get by with the most basic technologies; a ship would bring you work, a gun would help you keep it. A captain's goal was simple: find a crew, find a job, keep flying.

Art by Tim Bradstreet
Colors by Grant Goleash

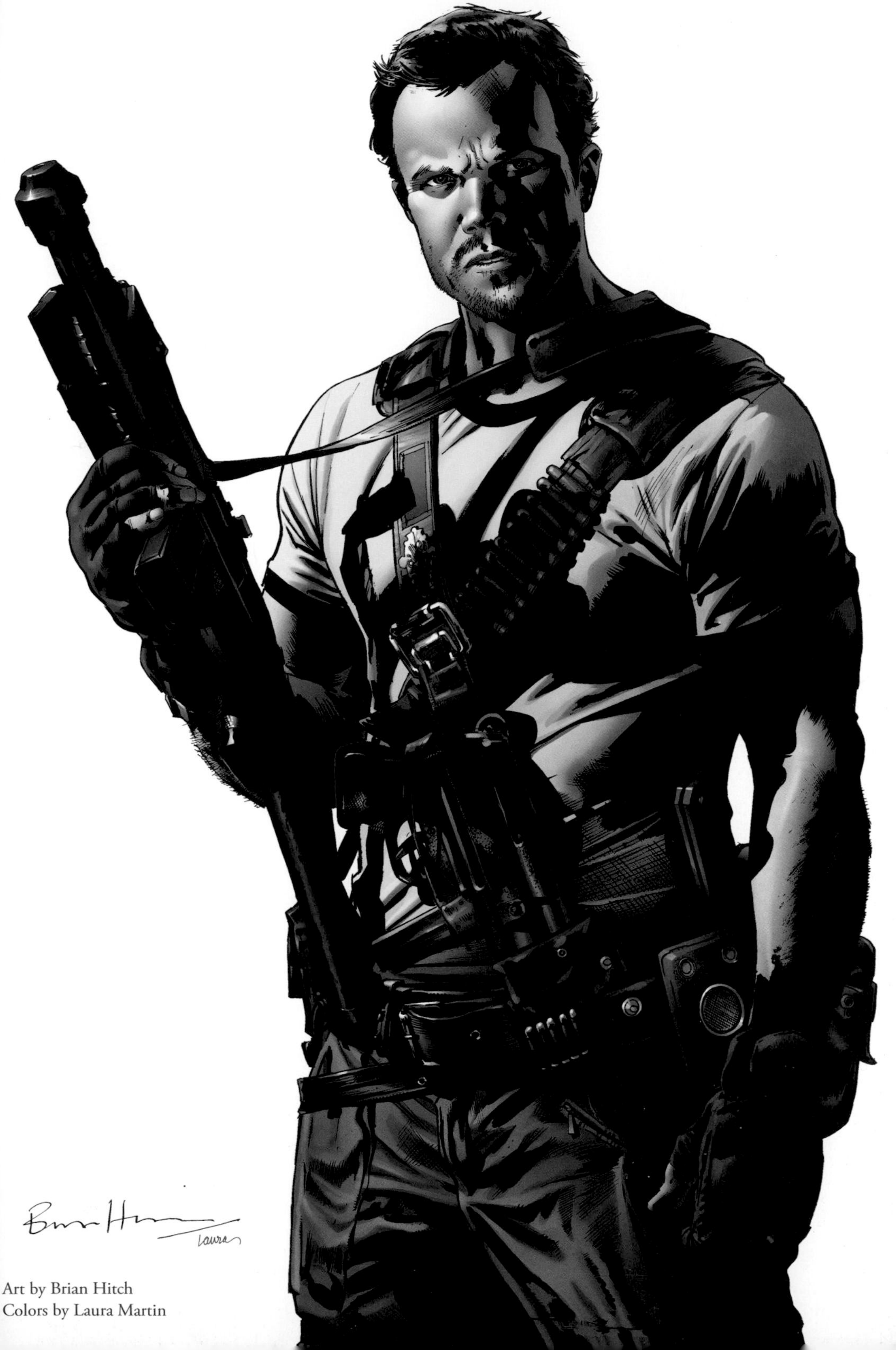

Art by Brian Hitch
Colors by Laura Martin

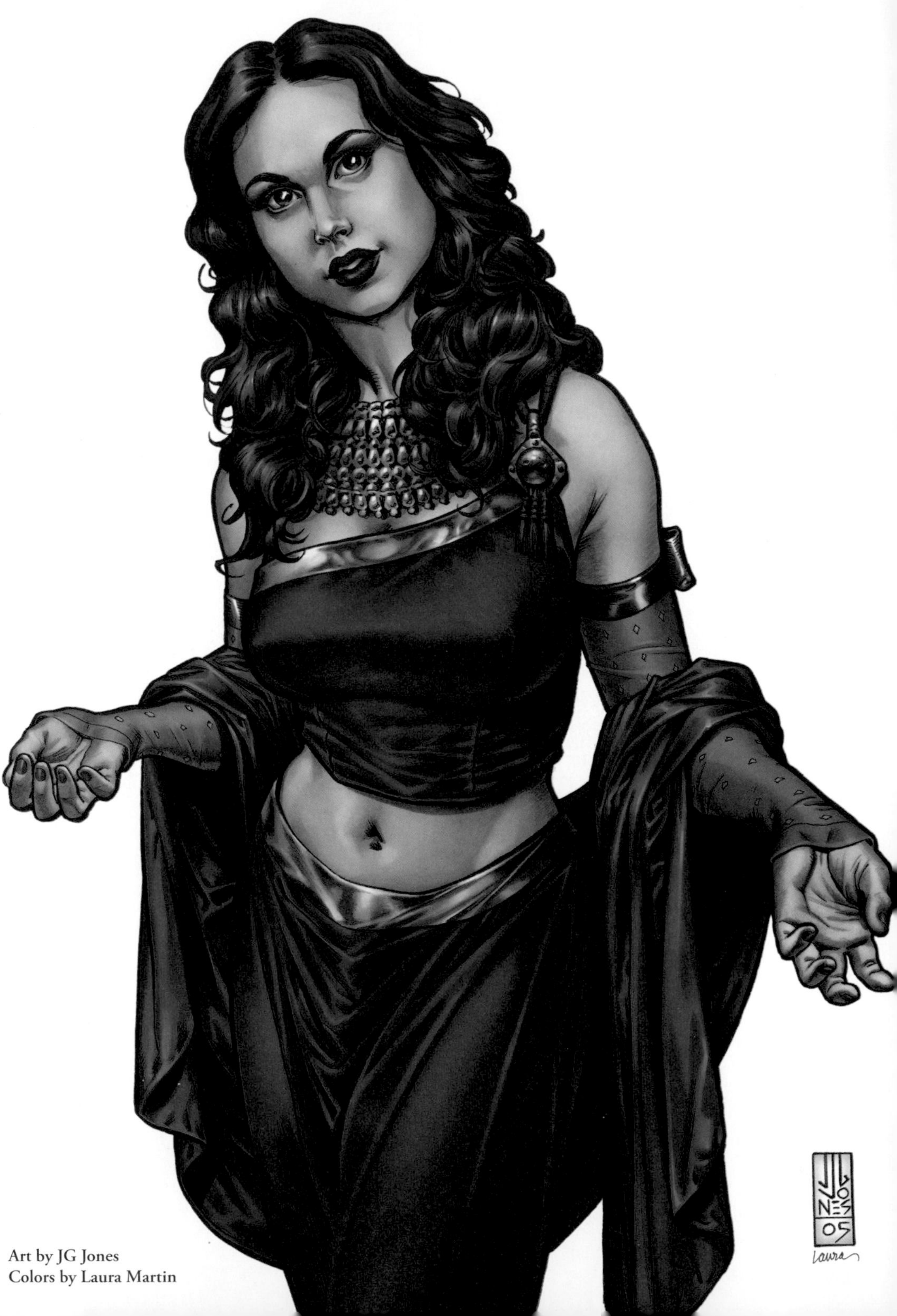
JG JONES 05
laura

Art by JG Jones
Colors by Laura Martin

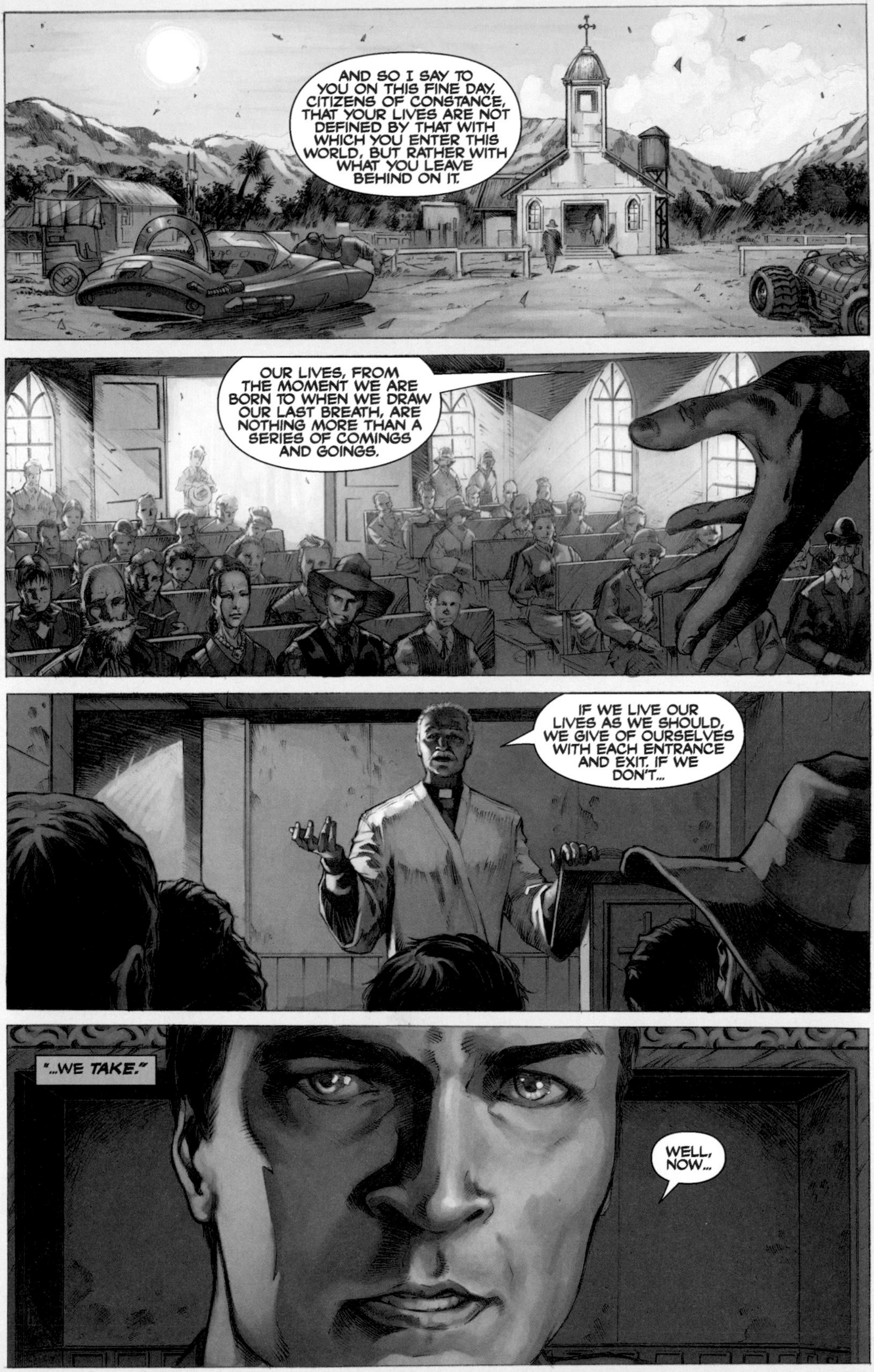
AND SO I SAY TO YOU ON THIS FINE DAY, CITIZENS OF CONSTANCE, THAT YOUR LIVES ARE NOT DEFINED BY THAT WITH WHICH YOU ENTER THIS WORLD, BUT RATHER WITH WHAT YOU LEAVE BEHIND ON IT.
OUR LIVES, FROM THE MOMENT WE ARE BORN TO WHEN WE DRAW OUR LAST BREATH, ARE NOTHING MORE THAN A SERIES OF COMINGS AND GOINGS.
IF WE LIVE OUR LIVES AS WE SHOULD, WE GIVE OF OURSELVES WITH EACH ENTRANCE AND EXIT. IF WE DON'T...
"...WE *TAKE*."
WELL, NOW...

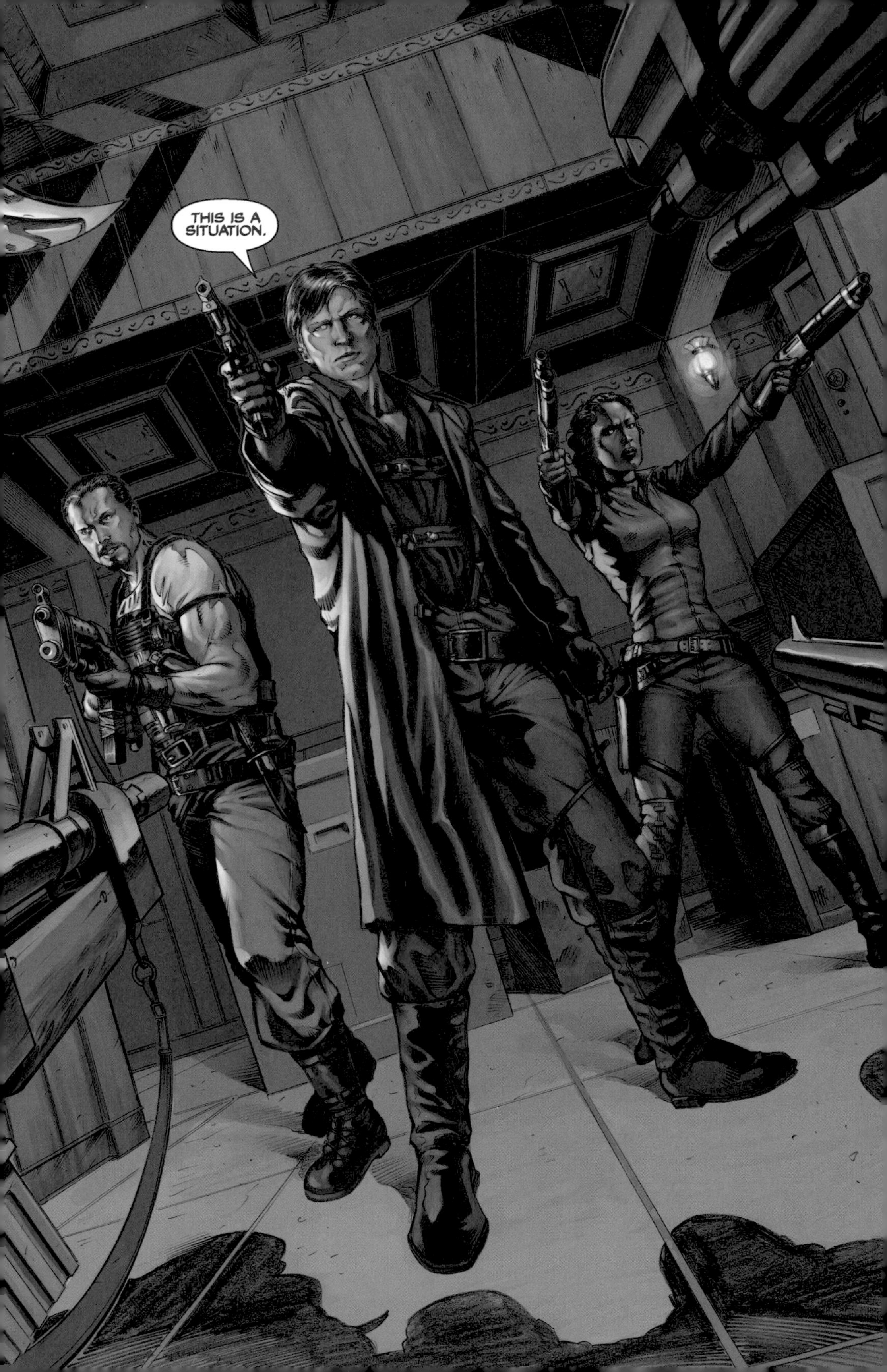
THIS IS A SITUATION.

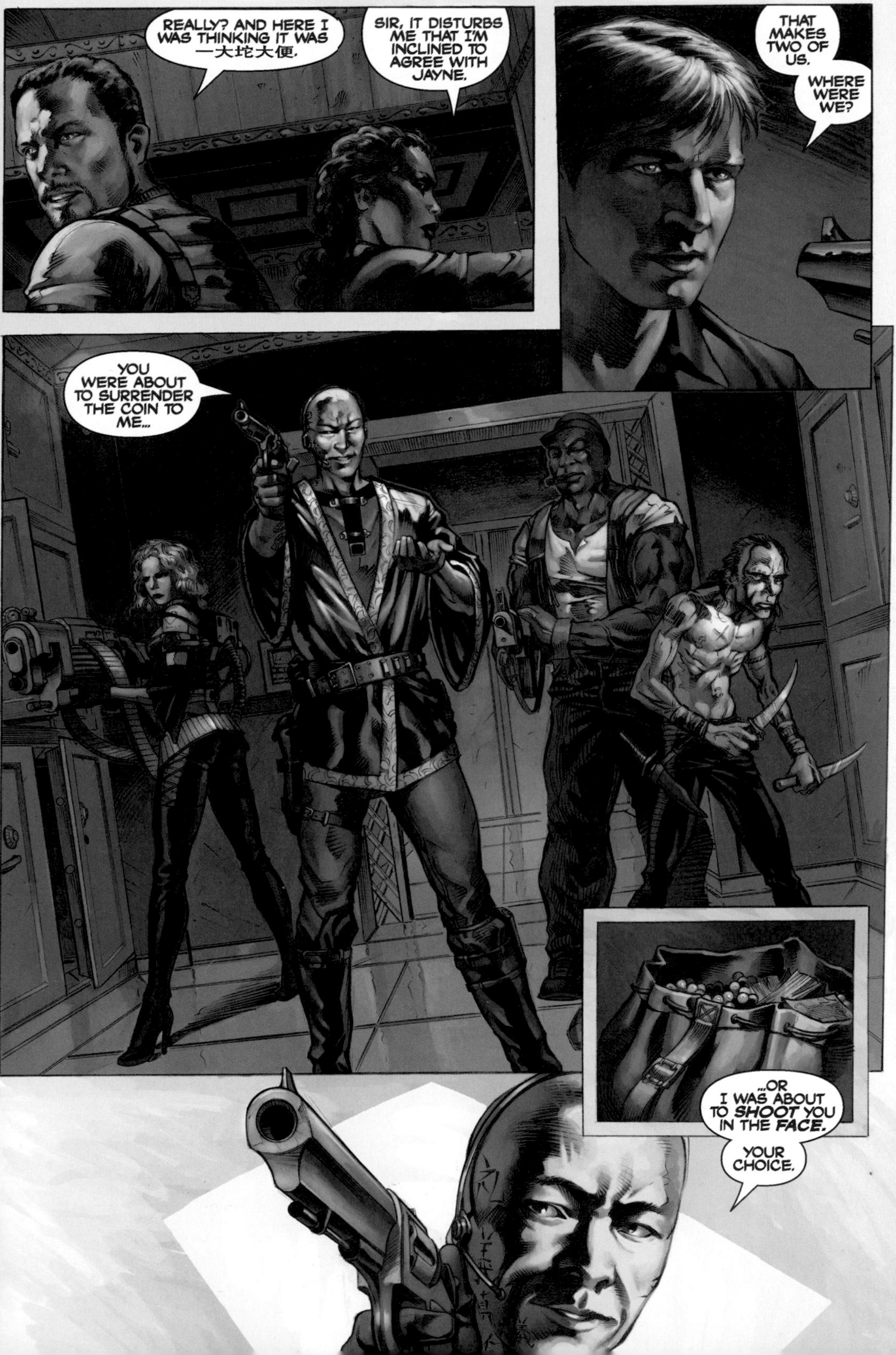
REALLY? AND HERE I WAS THINKING IT WAS 一大坨大便.
SIR, IT DISTURBS ME THAT I'M INCLINED TO AGREE WITH JAYNE.
THAT MAKES TWO OF US.
WHERE WERE WE?
YOU WERE ABOUT TO SURRENDER THE COIN TO ME...
...OR I WAS ABOUT TO *SHOOT* YOU IN THE *FACE.*
YOUR CHOICE.

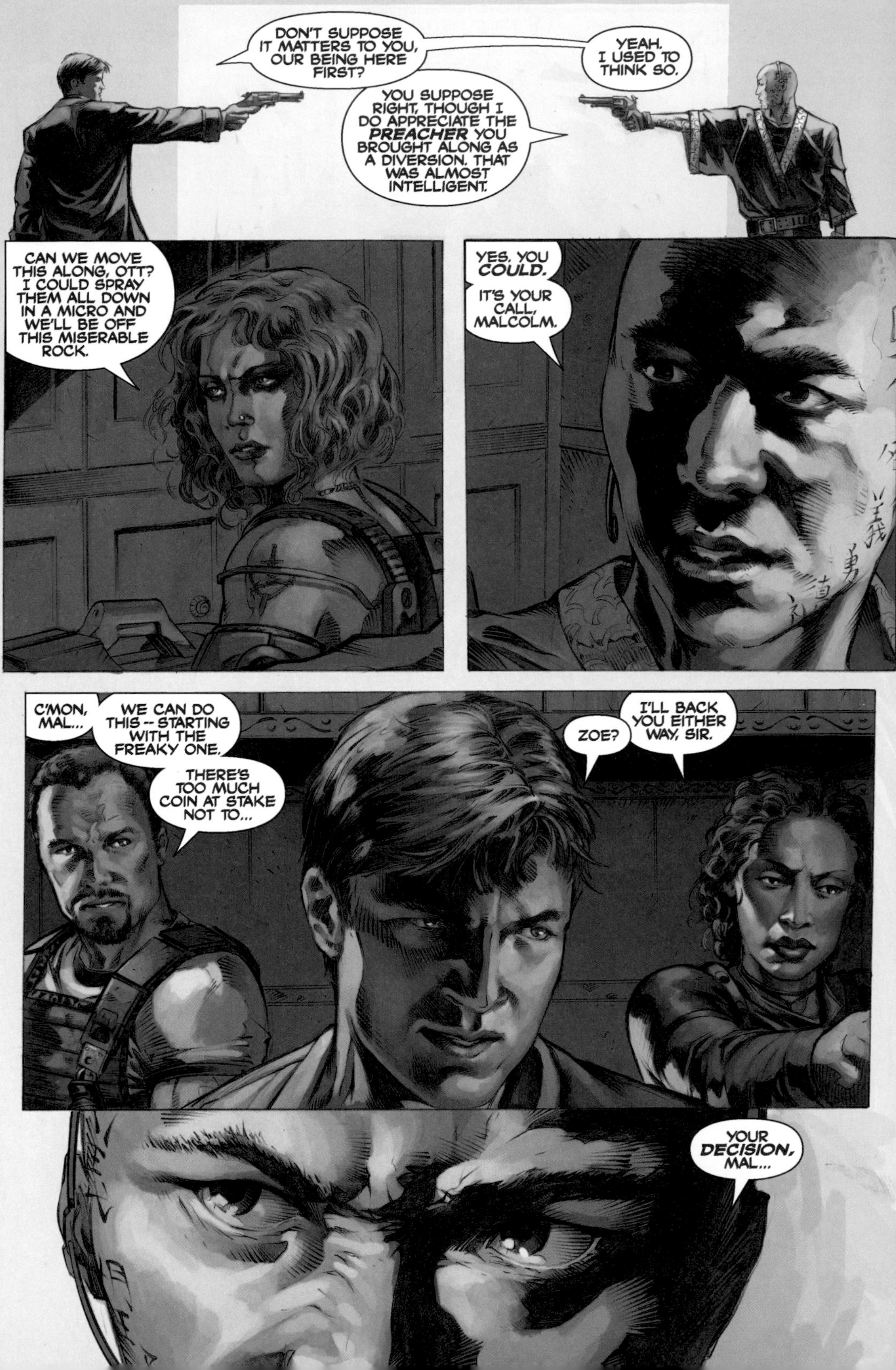
DON'T SUPPOSE IT MATTERS TO YOU, OUR BEING HERE FIRST?
YEAH. I USED TO THINK SO.
YOU SUPPOSE RIGHT, THOUGH I DO APPRECIATE THE PREACHER YOU BROUGHT ALONG AS A DIVERSION. THAT WAS ALMOST INTELLIGENT.
CAN WE MOVE THIS ALONG, OTT? I COULD SPRAY THEM ALL DOWN IN A MICRO AND WE'LL BE OFF THIS MISERABLE ROCK.
YES, YOU COULD.
IT'S YOUR CALL, MALCOLM.
C'MON, MAL...
WE CAN DO THIS -- STARTING WITH THE FREAKY ONE.
THERE'S TOO MUCH COIN AT STAKE NOT TO...
ZOE?
I'LL BACK YOU EITHER WAY, SIR.
YOUR DECISION, MAL...

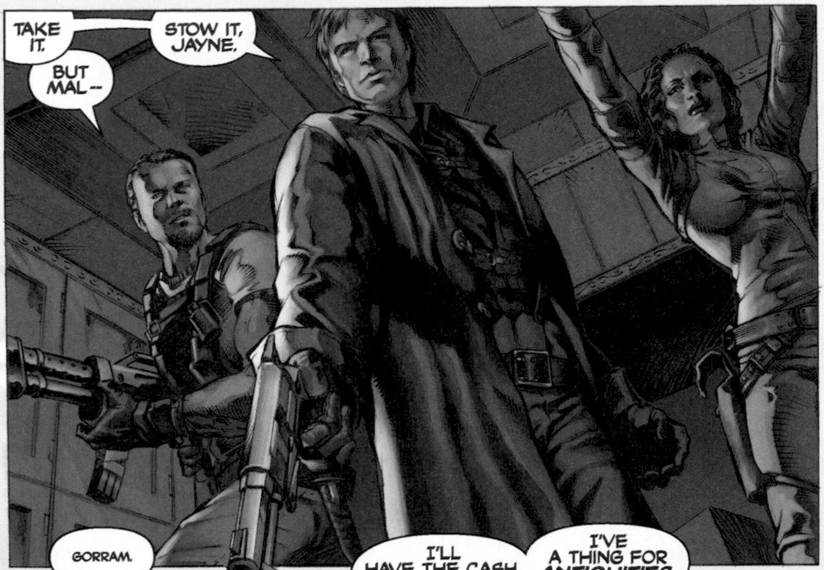
TAKE IT.
STOW IT, JAYNE.
BUT MAL--
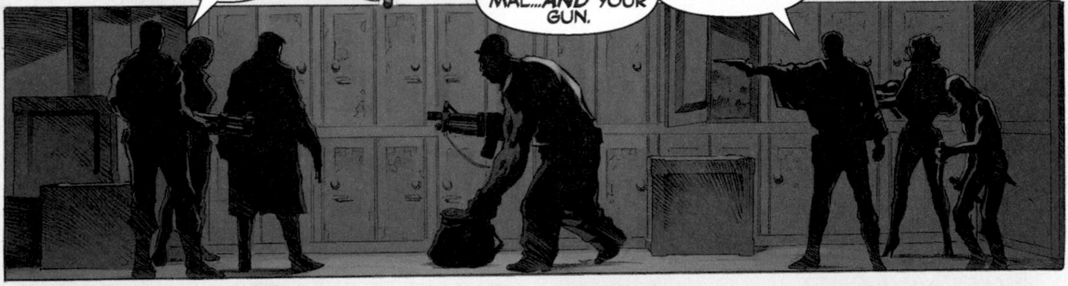
GORRAM.
I'LL HAVE THE CASH, MAL...AND YOUR GUN.
I'VE A THING FOR ANTIQUITIES.
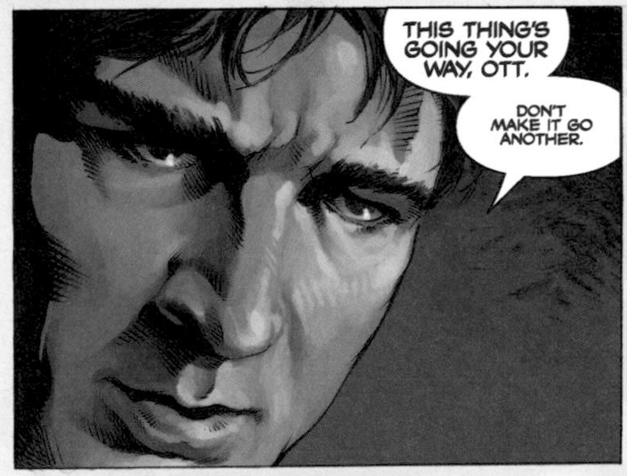
THIS THING'S GOING YOUR WAY, OTT.
DON'T MAKE IT GO ANOTHER.
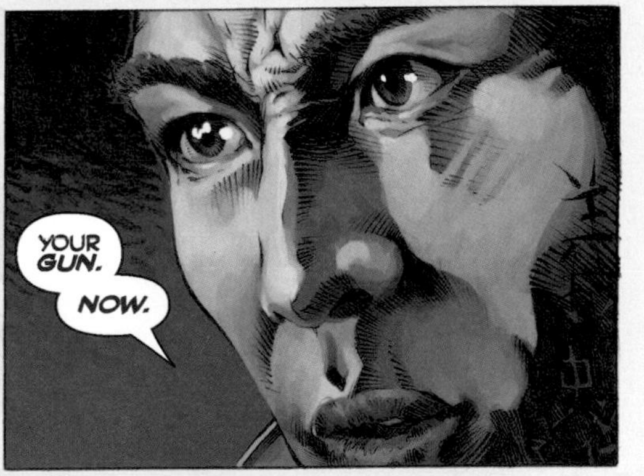
YOUR GUN.
NOW.
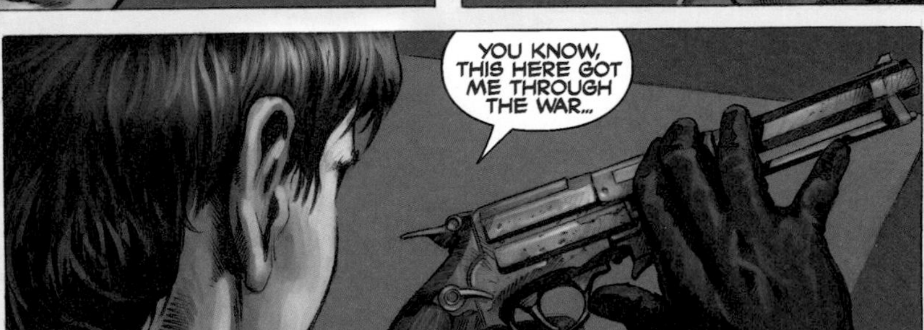
YOU KNOW, THIS HERE GOT ME THROUGH THE WAR...

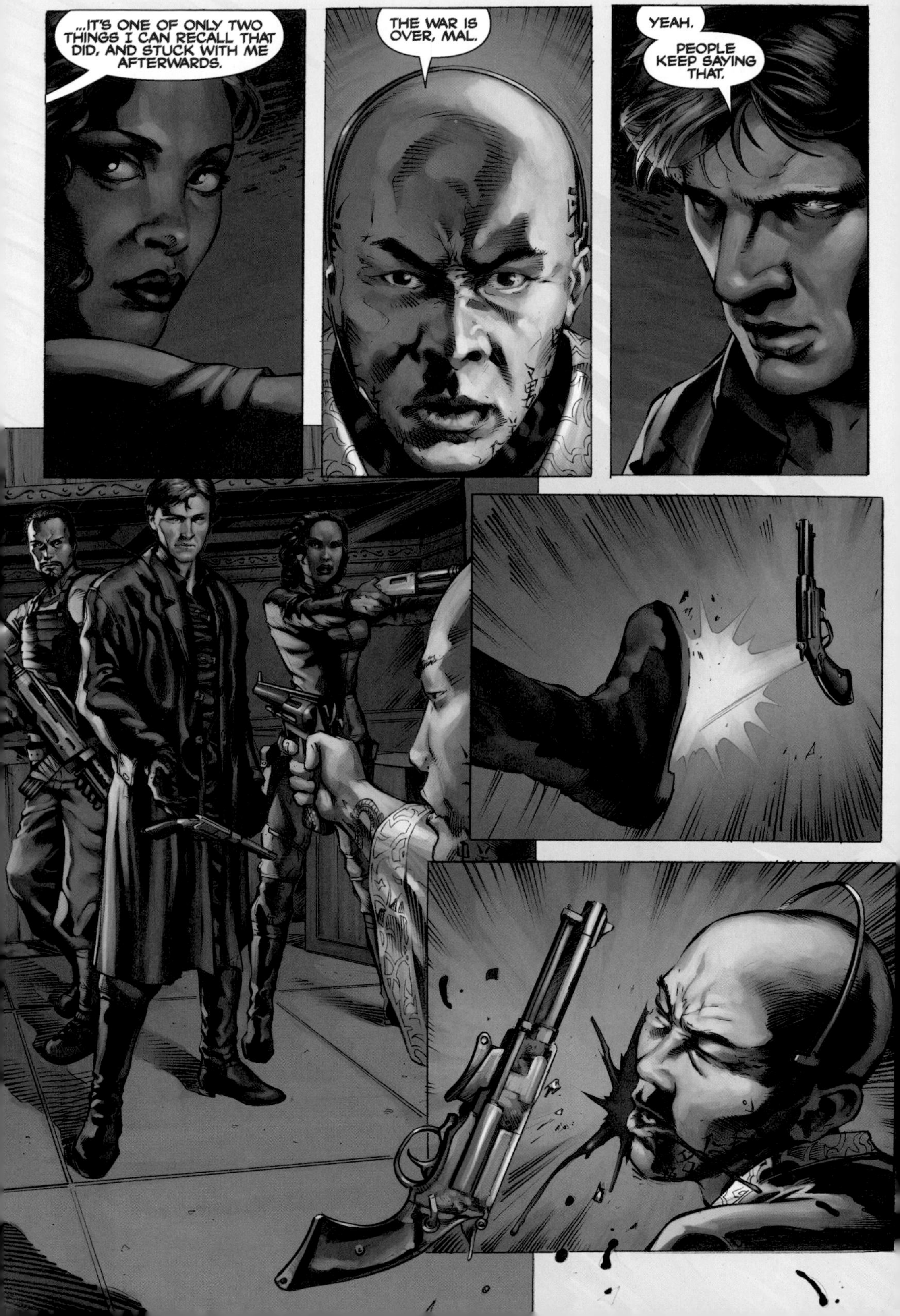
...IT'S ONE OF ONLY TWO THINGS I CAN RECALL THAT DID, AND STUCK WITH ME AFTERWARDS.
THE WAR IS OVER, MAL.
YEAH.
PEOPLE KEEP SAYING THAT.

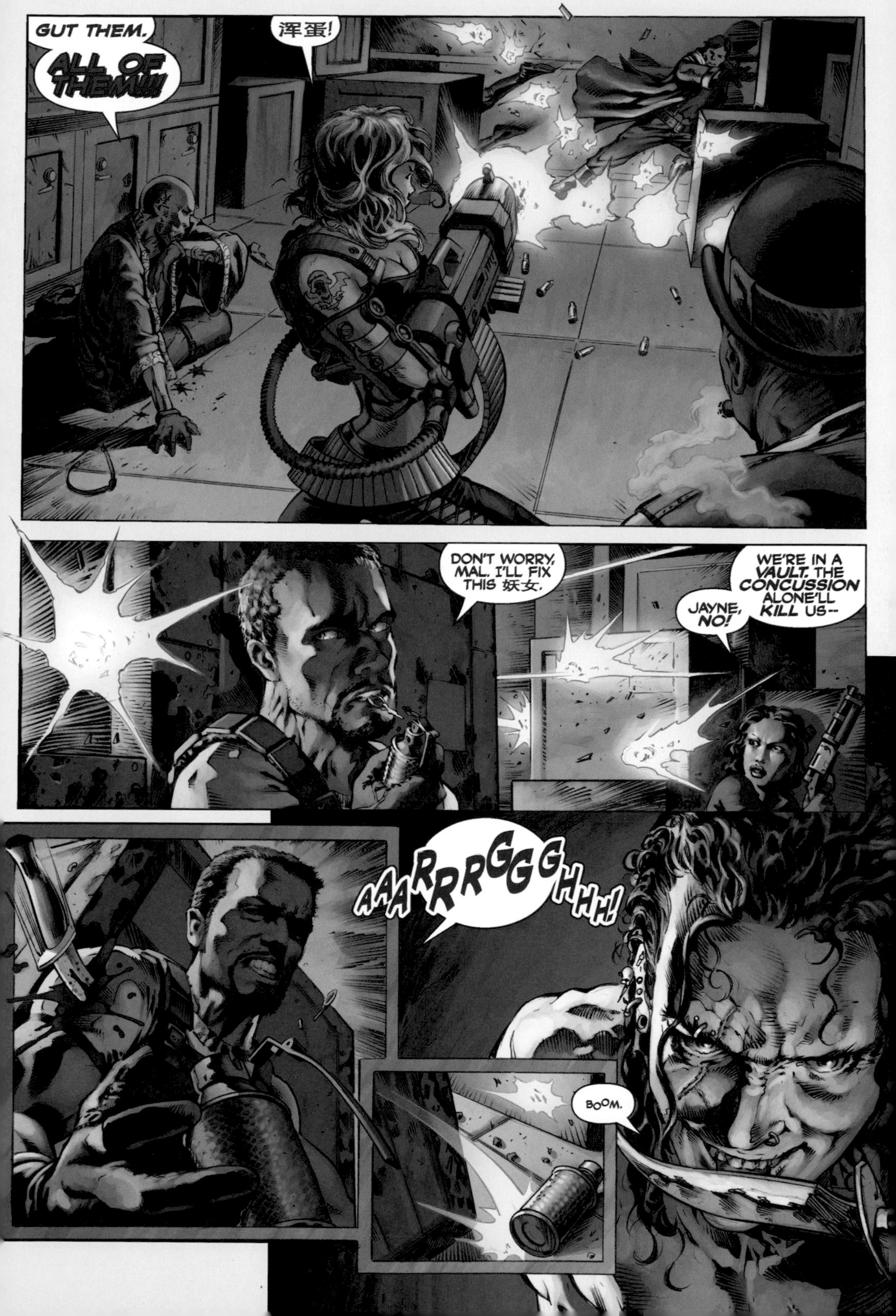
GUT THEM.
ALL OF THEM!!!
浑蛋!
DON'T WORRY, MAL. I'LL FIX THIS 妖女.
WE'RE IN A VAULT. THE CONCUSSION ALONE'LL KILL US--
JAYNE, NO!
AAARRRGGGHHH!
BOOM.

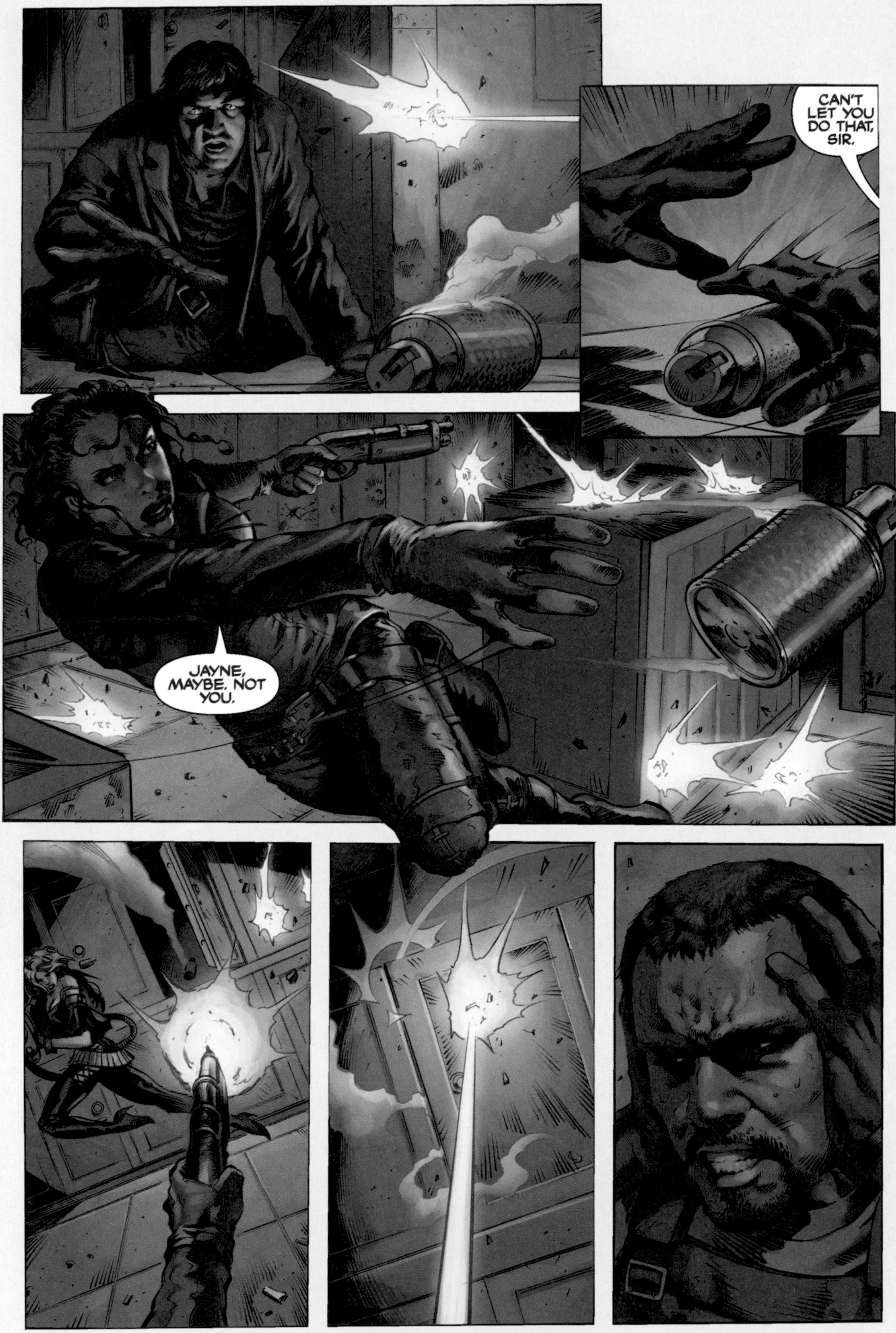
CAN'T LET YOU DO THAT, SIR.
JAYNE, MAYBE. NOT YOU.

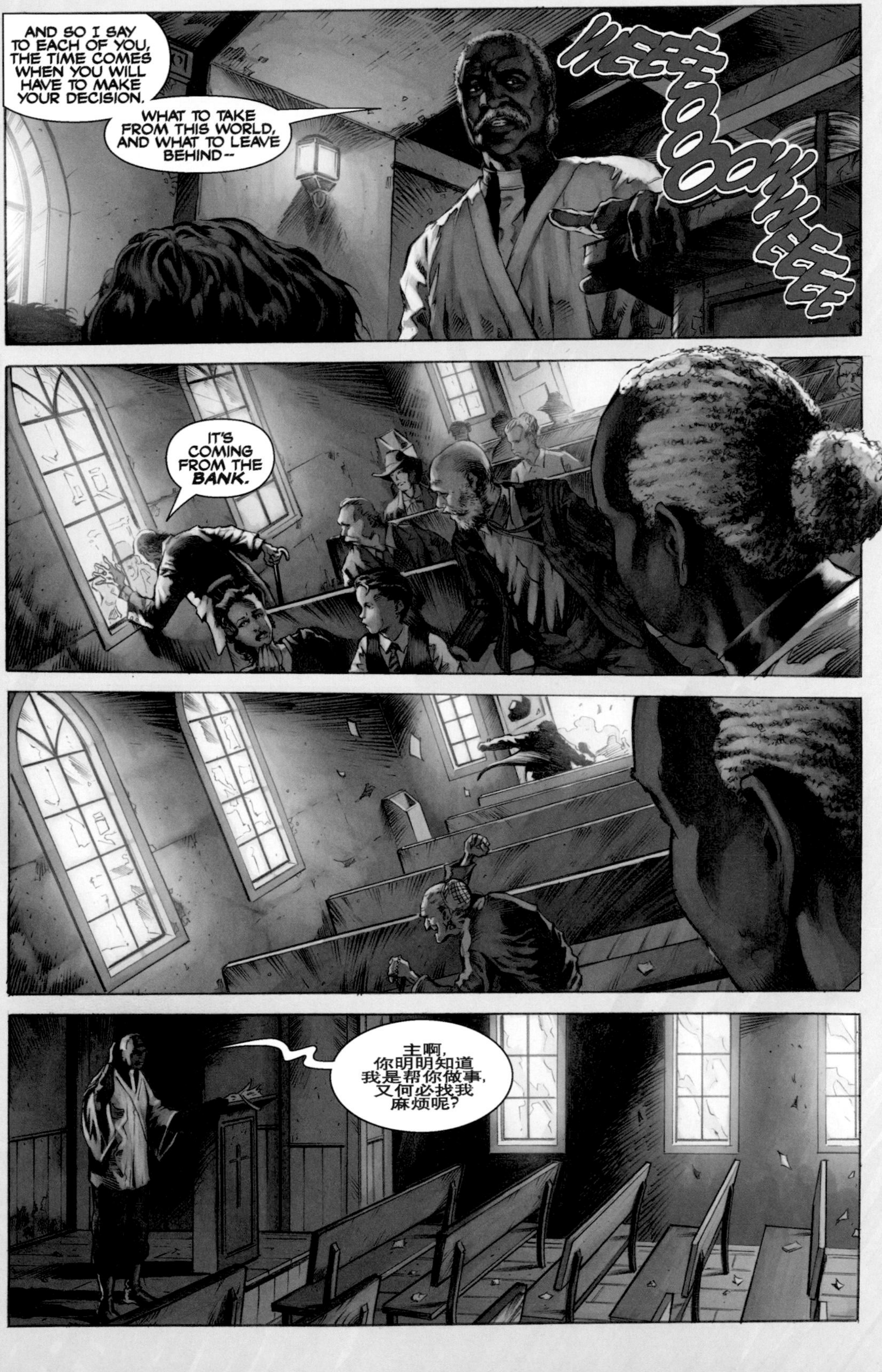
AND SO I SAY TO EACH OF YOU, THE TIME COMES WHEN YOU WILL HAVE TO MAKE YOUR DECISION.
WHAT TO TAKE FROM THIS WORLD, AND WHAT TO LEAVE BEHIND--
WEEEEOOOOWEEEE
IT'S COMING FROM THE BANK.
主啊，你明明知道我是帮你做事，又何必找我麻烦呢？

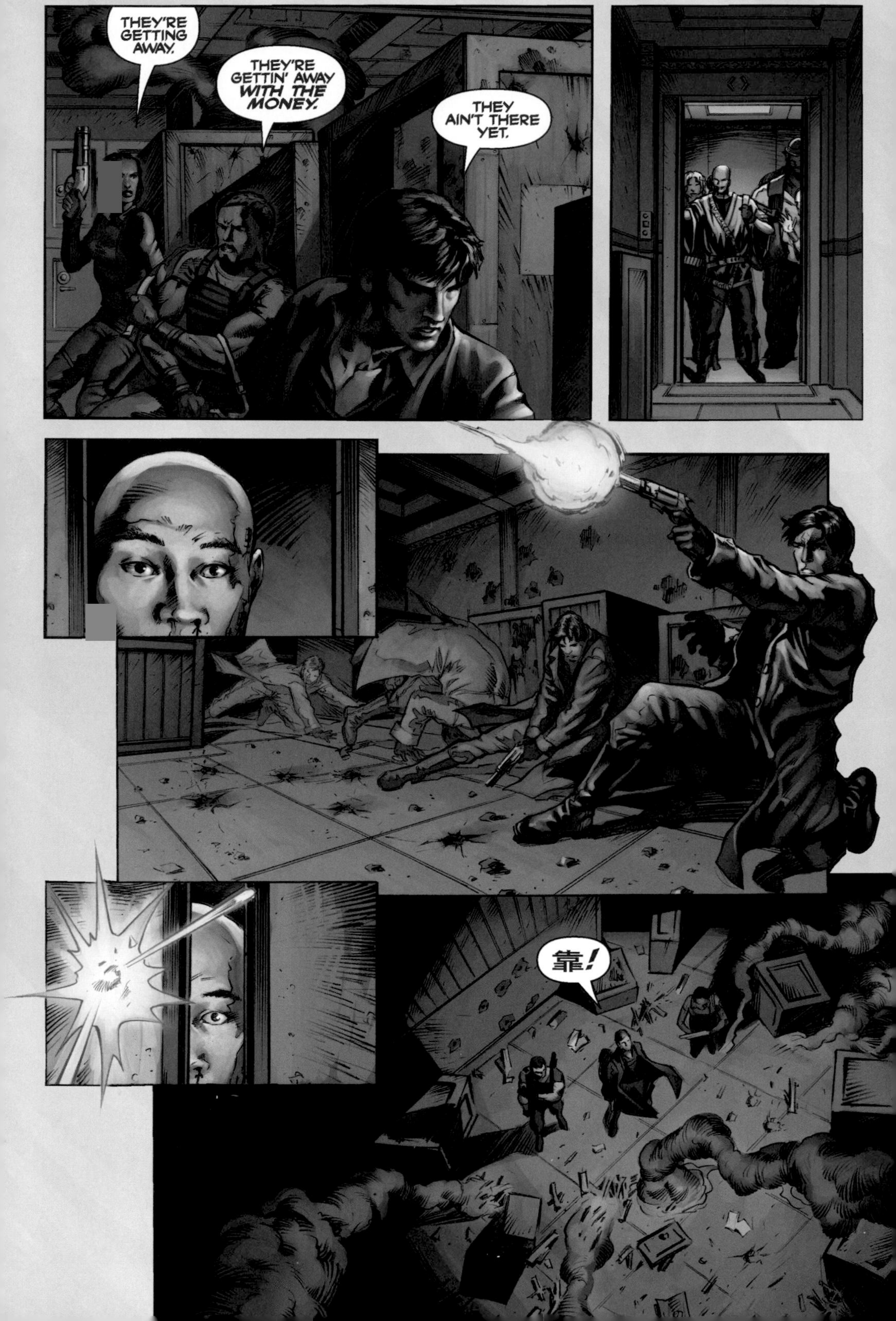
THEY'RE GETTING AWAY.
THEY'RE GETTIN' AWAY *WITH THE MONEY.*
THEY AIN'T THERE YET.
靠!

GONNA TAKE A WHILE FOR THE STINK OF THIS TO PASS.

JUST A SEWER, JAYNE.

WEREN'T TALKING ABOUT THE SEWER.

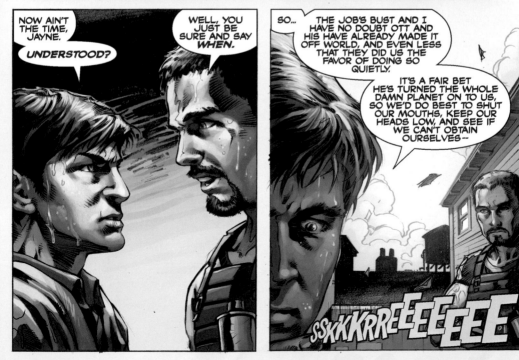

NOW AIN'T THE TIME, JAYNE.

UNDERSTOOD?

WELL, YOU JUST BE SURE AND SAY *WHEN.*

SO...

THE JOB'S BUST AND I HAVE NO DOUBT OTT AND HIS HAVE ALREADY MADE IT OFF WORLD, AND EVEN LESS THAT THEY DID US THE FAVOR OF DOING SO QUIETLY.

IT'S A FAIR BET HE'S TURNED THE WHOLE DAMN PLANET ON TO US, SO WE'D DO BEST TO SHUT OUR MOUTHS, KEEP OUR HEADS LOW, AND SEE IF WE CAN'T OBTAIN OURSELVES--

SSKKKRREEEEEEE

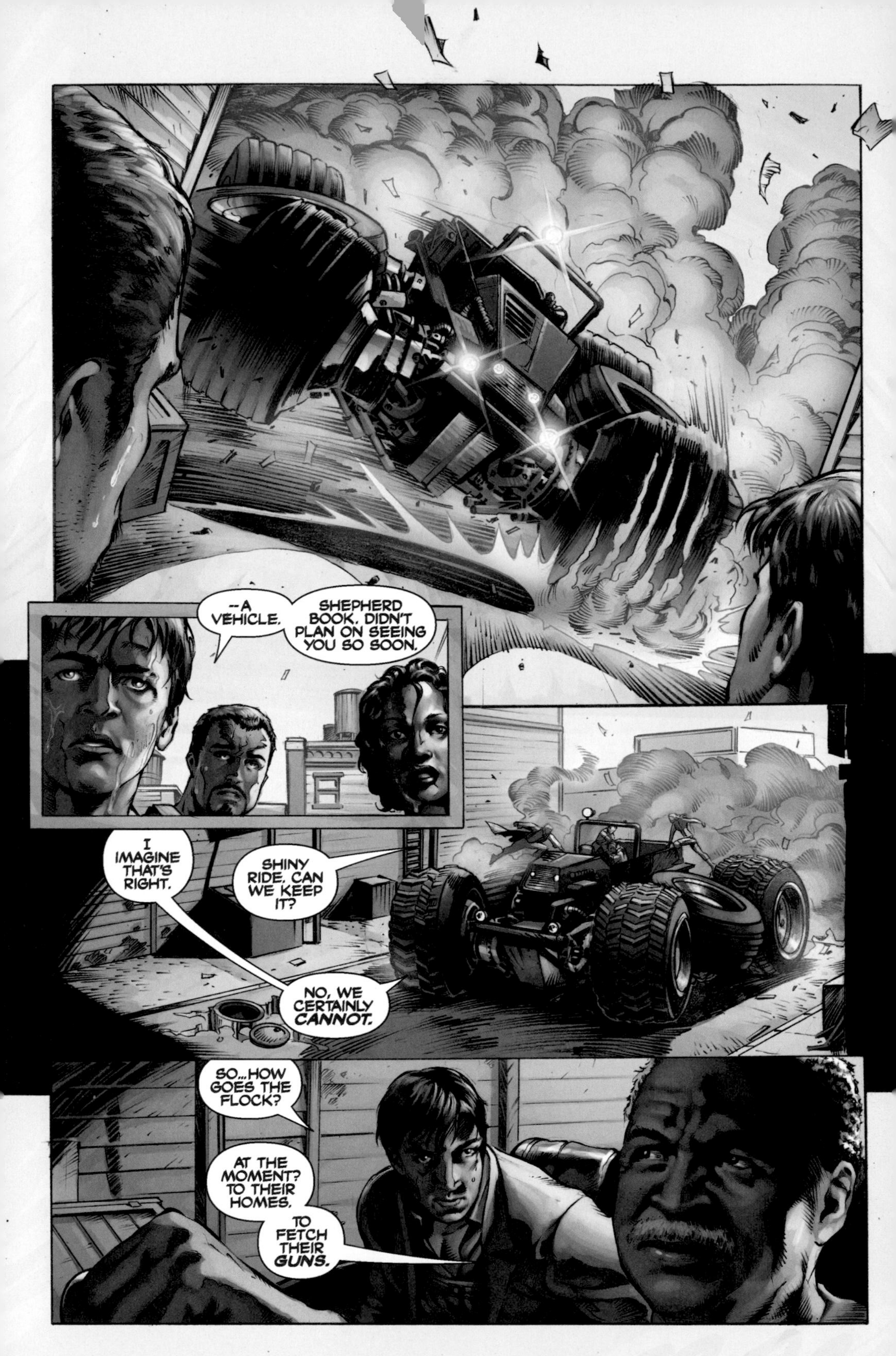
--A VEHICLE.
SHEPHERD BOOK. DIDN'T PLAN ON SEEING YOU SO SOON.
I IMAGINE THAT'S RIGHT.
SHINY RIDE. CAN WE KEEP IT?
NO, WE CERTAINLY *CANNOT.*
SO...HOW GOES THE FLOCK?
AT THE MOMENT? TO THEIR HOMES.
TO FETCH THEIR *GUNS.*

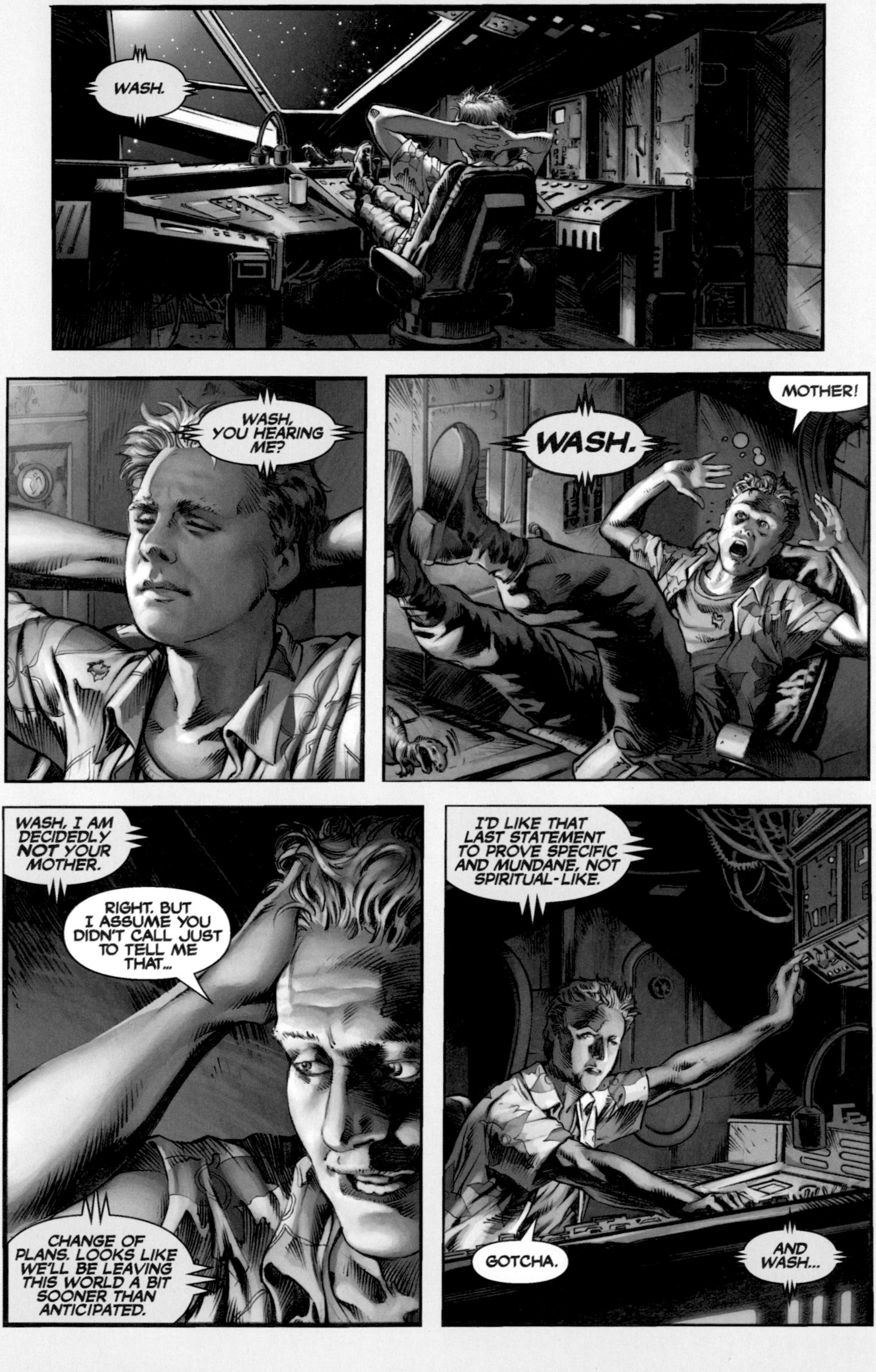
WASH.
WASH, YOU HEARING ME?
WASH.
MOTHER!
WASH, I AM DECIDEDLY NOT YOUR MOTHER.
RIGHT, BUT I ASSUME YOU DIDN'T CALL JUST TO TELL ME THAT...
CHANGE OF PLANS. LOOKS LIKE WE'LL BE LEAVING THIS WORLD A BIT SOONER THAN ANTICIPATED.
I'D LIKE THAT LAST STATEMENT TO PROVE SPECIFIC AND MUNDANE, NOT SPIRITUAL-LIKE.
GOTCHA.
AND WASH...

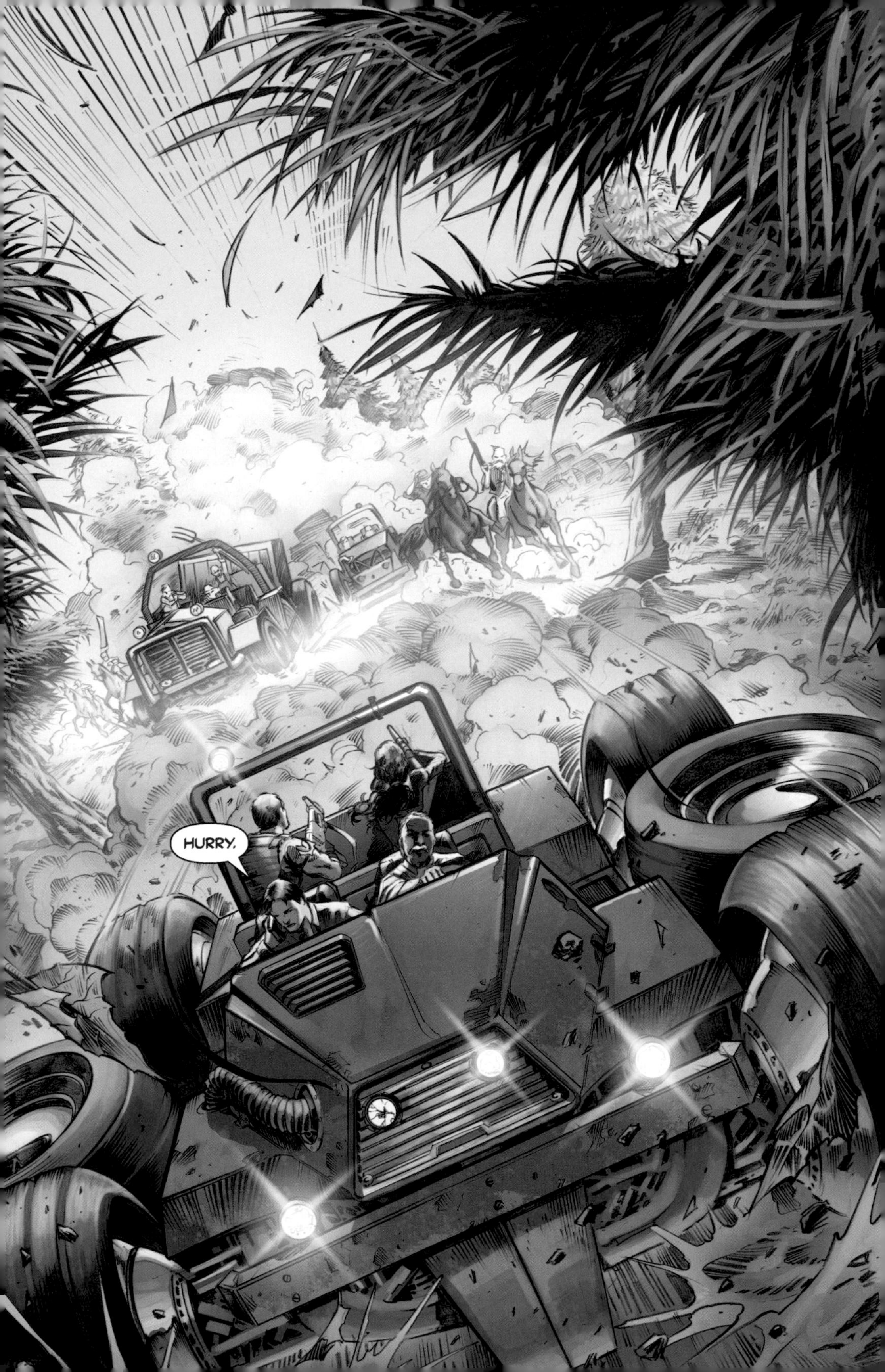
HURRY.

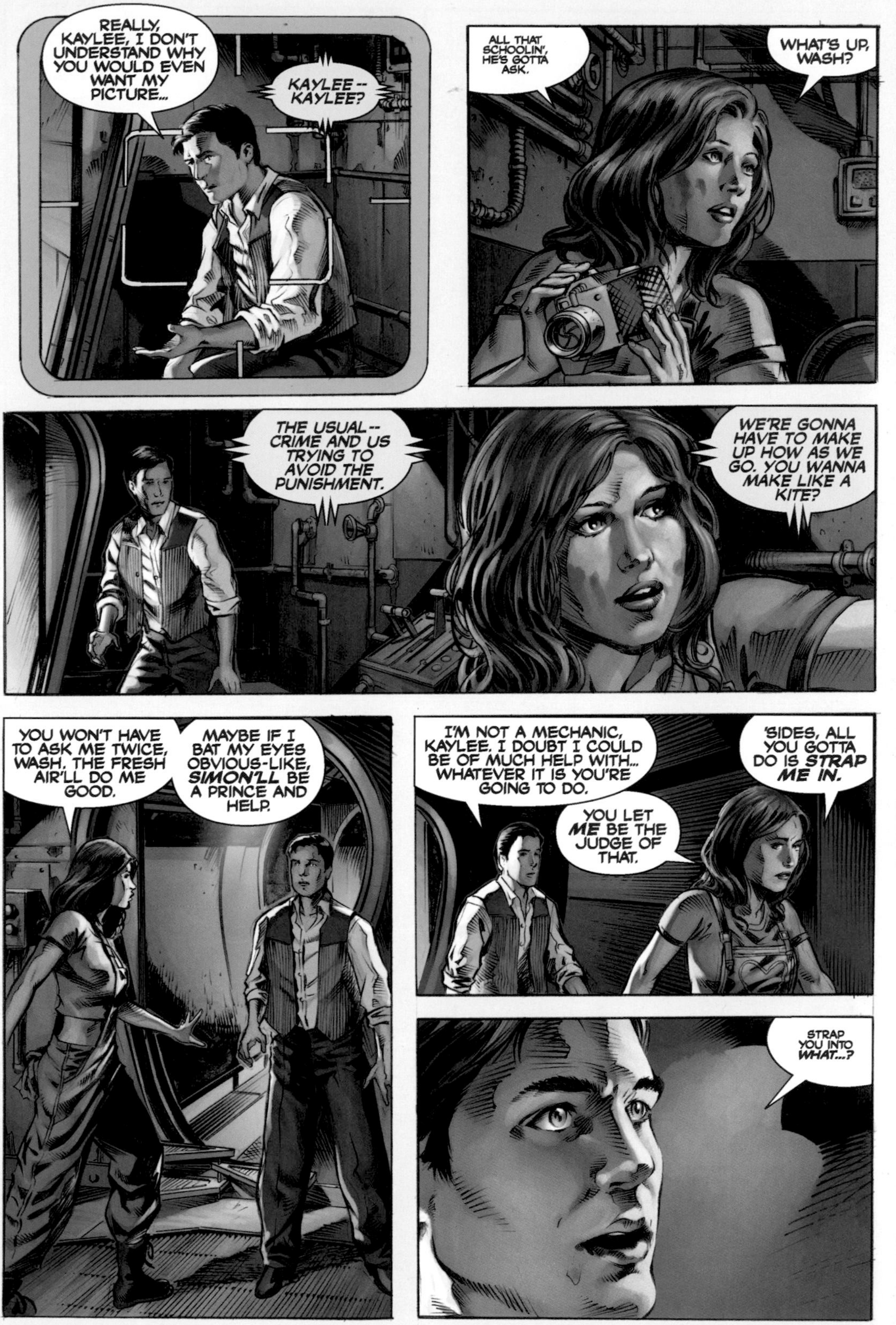
REALLY, KAYLEE, I DON'T UNDERSTAND WHY YOU WOULD EVEN WANT MY PICTURE...
KAYLEE -- KAYLEE?
ALL THAT SCHOOLIN', HE'S GOTTA ASK.
WHAT'S UP, WASH?
THE USUAL -- CRIME AND US TRYING TO AVOID THE PUNISHMENT.
WE'RE GONNA HAVE TO MAKE UP HOW AS WE GO. YOU WANNA MAKE LIKE A KITE?
YOU WON'T HAVE TO ASK ME TWICE, WASH. THE FRESH AIR'LL DO ME GOOD.
MAYBE IF I BAT MY EYES OBVIOUS-LIKE, SIMON'LL BE A PRINCE AND HELP.
I'M NOT A MECHANIC, KAYLEE. I DOUBT I COULD BE OF MUCH HELP WITH... WHATEVER IT IS YOU'RE GOING TO DO.
YOU LET ME BE THE JUDGE OF THAT.
'SIDES, ALL YOU GOTTA DO IS STRAP ME IN.
STRAP YOU INTO WHAT...?

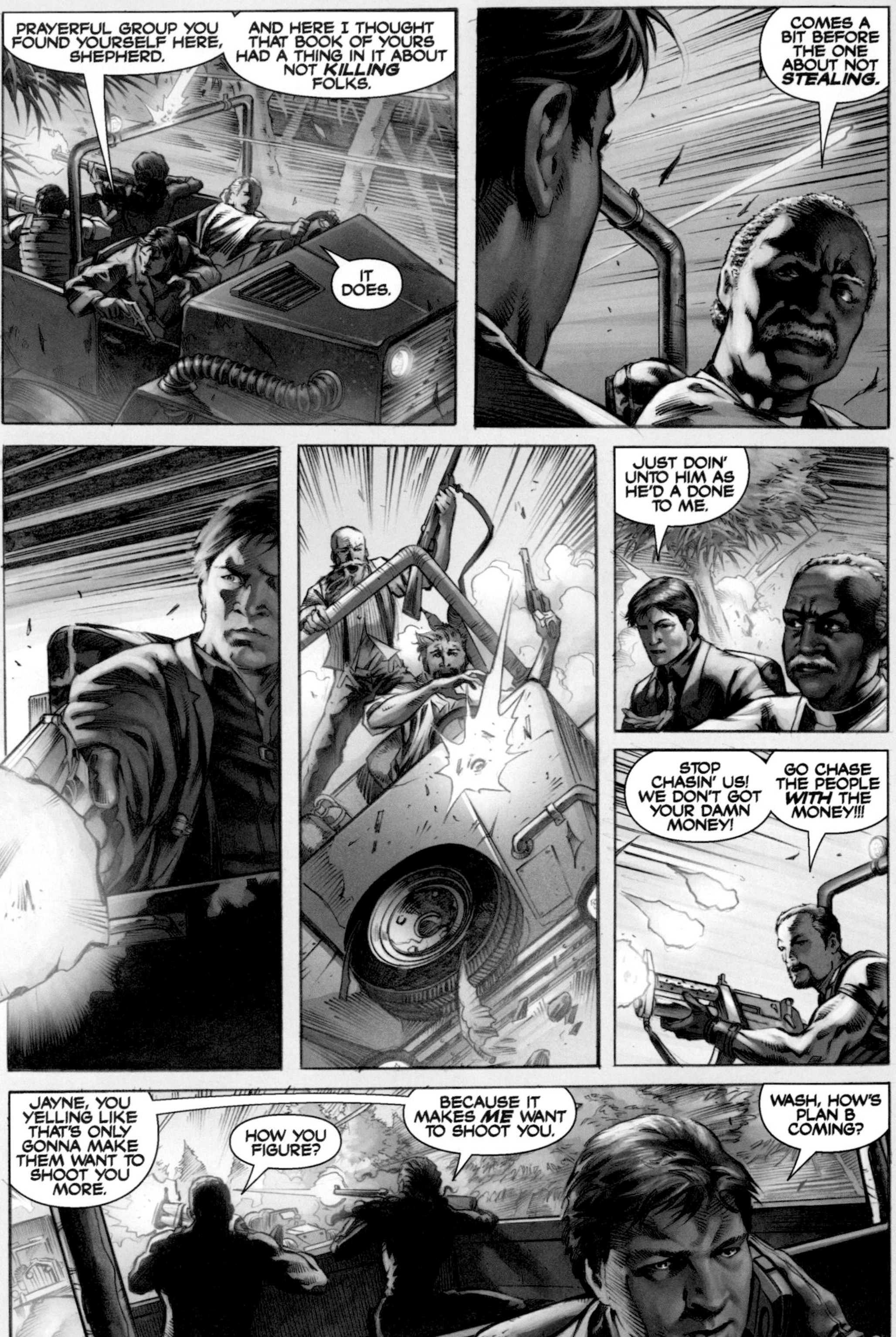
PRAYERFUL GROUP YOU FOUND YOURSELF HERE, SHEPHERD.
AND HERE I THOUGHT THAT BOOK OF YOURS HAD A THING IN IT ABOUT NOT KILLING FOLKS.
IT DOES.
COMES A BIT BEFORE THE ONE ABOUT NOT STEALING.
JUST DOIN' UNTO HIM AS HE'D A DONE TO ME.
STOP CHASIN' US! WE DON'T GOT YOUR DAMN MONEY!
GO CHASE THE PEOPLE WITH THE MONEY!!!
JAYNE, YOU YELLING LIKE THAT'S ONLY GONNA MAKE THEM WANT TO SHOOT YOU MORE.
HOW YOU FIGURE?
BECAUSE IT MAKES ME WANT TO SHOOT YOU.
WASH, HOW'S PLAN B COMING?

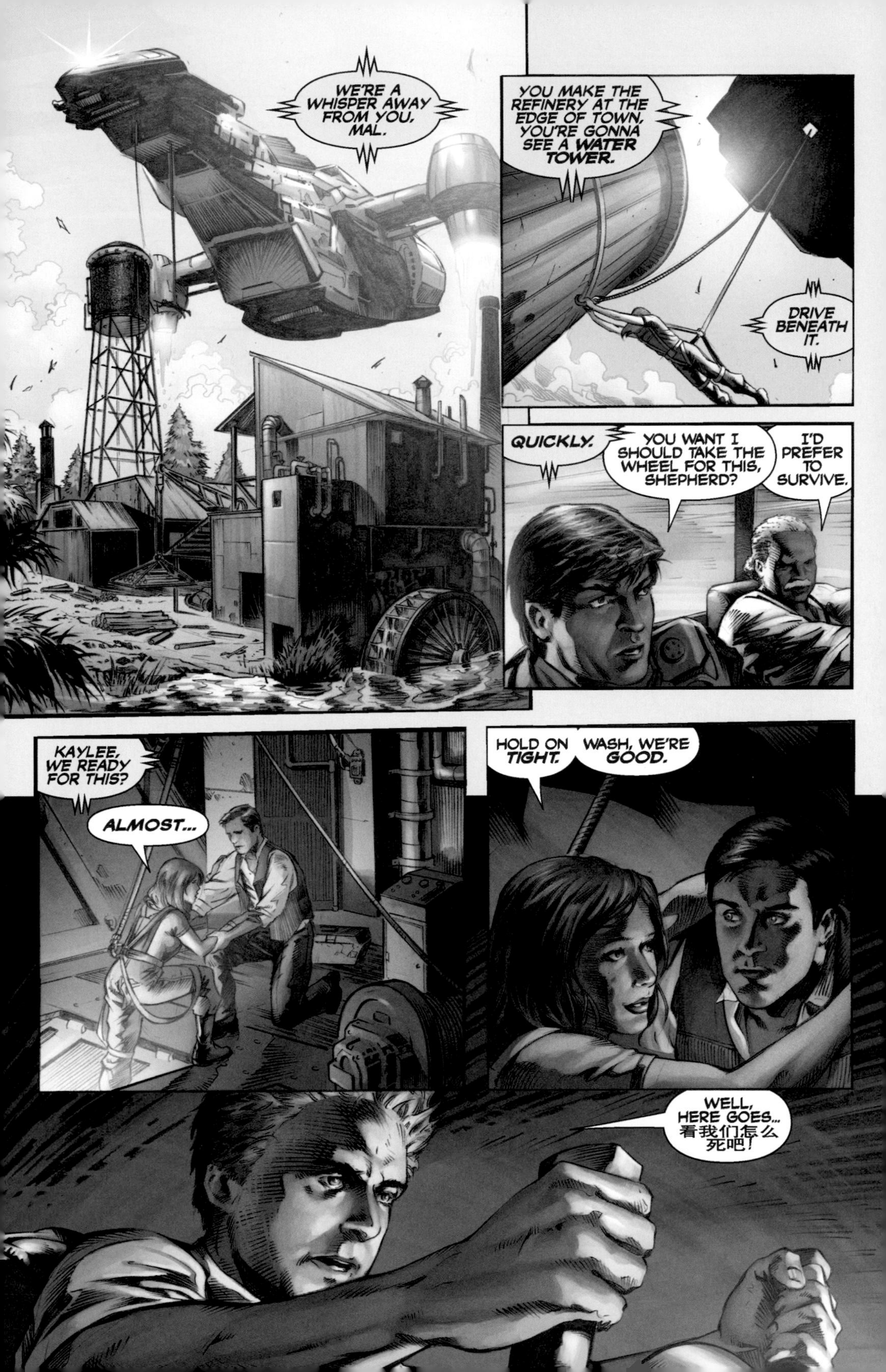
WE'RE A WHISPER AWAY FROM YOU, MAL.
YOU MAKE THE REFINERY AT THE EDGE OF TOWN, YOU'RE GONNA SEE A WATER TOWER.
DRIVE BENEATH IT.
QUICKLY.
YOU WANT I SHOULD TAKE THE WHEEL FOR THIS, SHEPHERD?
I'D PREFER TO SURVIVE.
KAYLEE, WE READY FOR THIS?
ALMOST...
HOLD ON TIGHT.
WASH, WE'RE GOOD.
WELL, HERE GOES... 看我们怎么死吧!

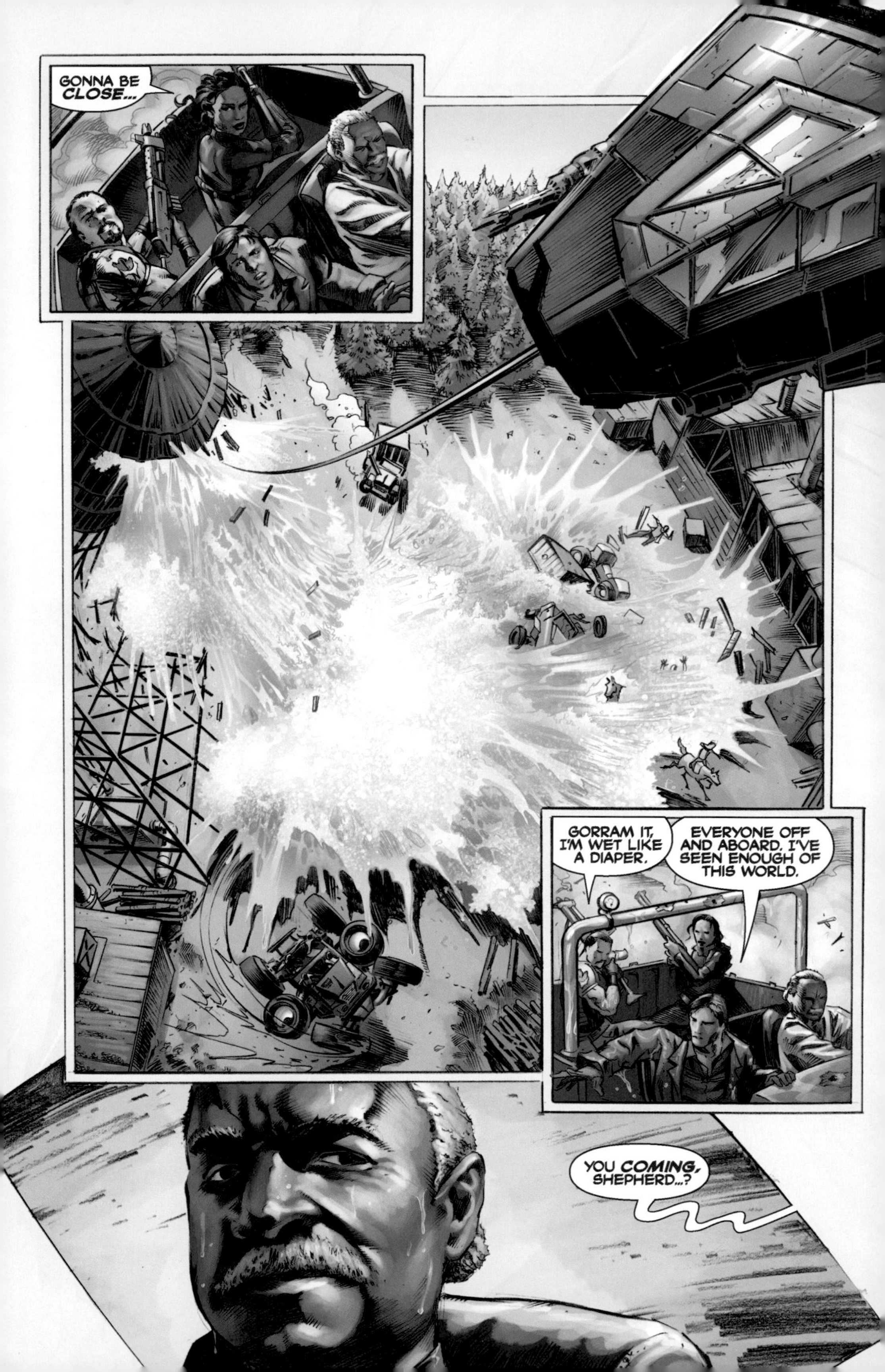
GONNA BE CLOSE...
GORRAM IT, I'M WET LIKE A DIAPER.
EVERYONE OFF AND ABOARD. I'VE SEEN ENOUGH OF THIS WORLD.
YOU COMING, SHEPHERD...?

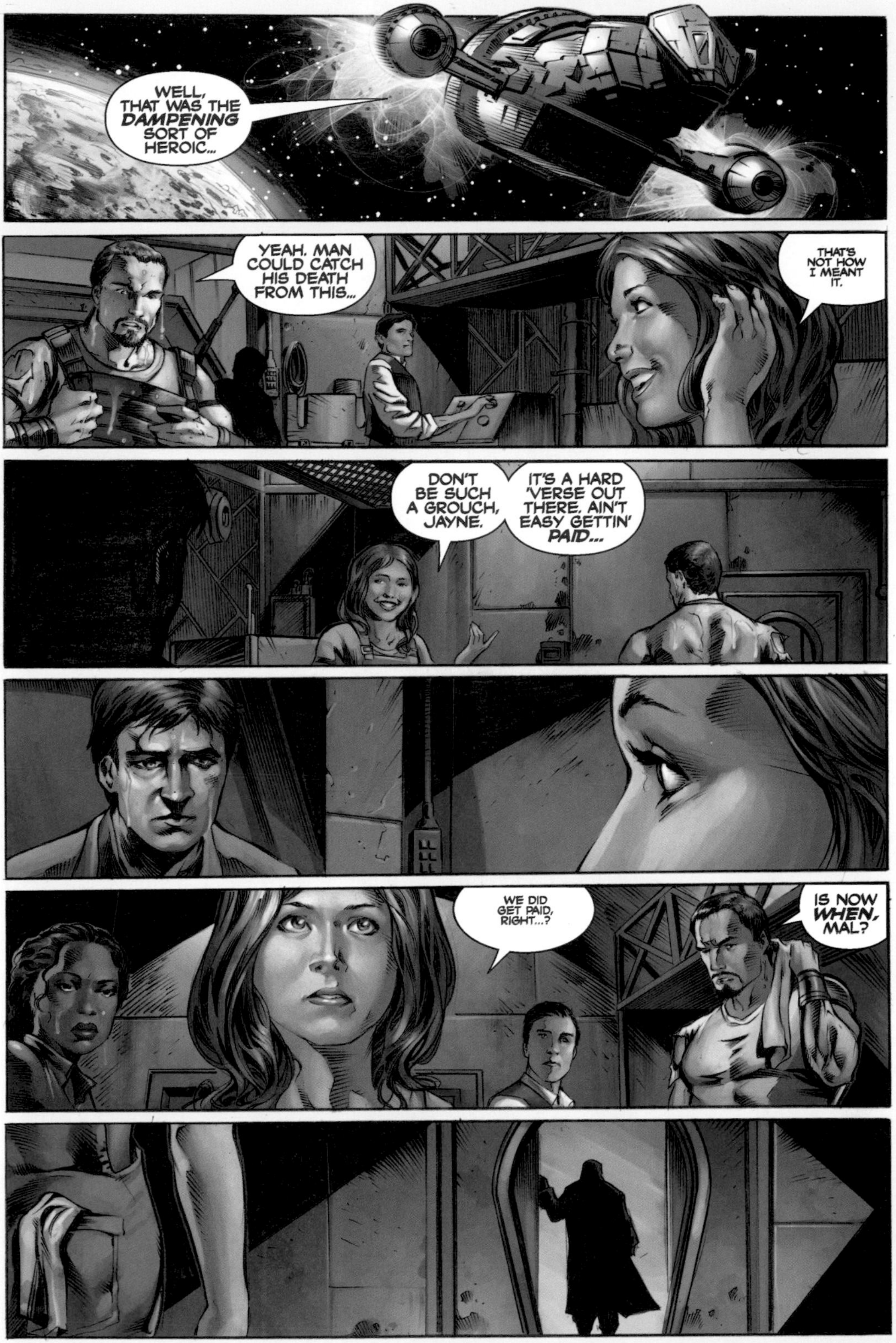
WELL, THAT WAS THE DAMPENING SORT OF HEROIC...
YEAH. MAN COULD CATCH HIS DEATH FROM THIS...
THAT'S NOT HOW I MEANT IT.
DON'T BE SUCH A GROUCH, JAYNE.
IT'S A HARD 'VERSE OUT THERE. AIN'T EASY GETTIN' PAID...
WE DID GET PAID, RIGHT...?
IS NOW WHEN, MAL?

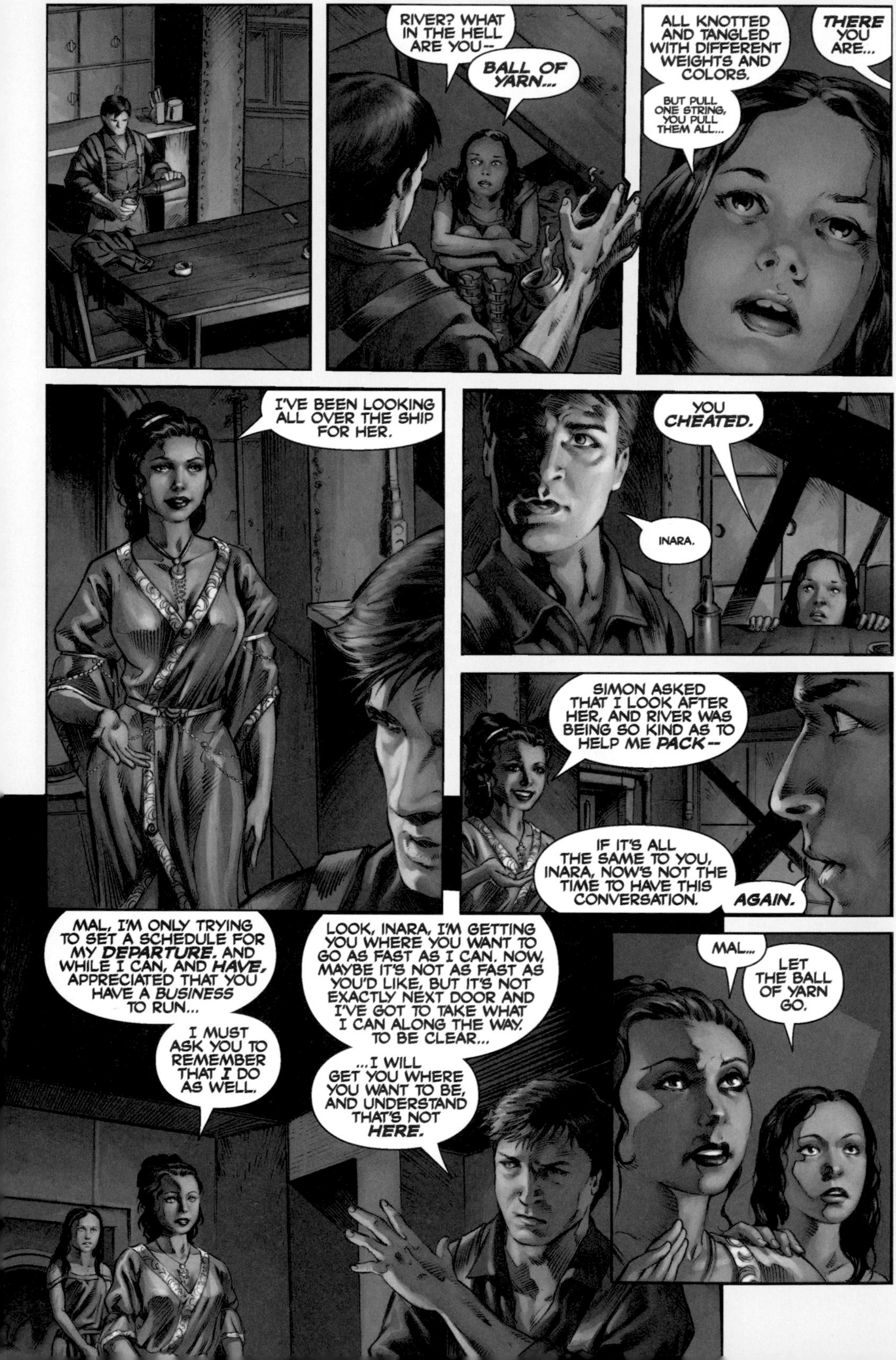
RIVER? WHAT IN THE HELL ARE YOU--
BALL OF YARN...
ALL KNOTTED AND TANGLED WITH DIFFERENT WEIGHTS AND COLORS.
BUT PULL ONE STRING, YOU PULL THEM ALL...
THERE YOU ARE...
I'VE BEEN LOOKING ALL OVER THE SHIP FOR HER.
YOU CHEATED.
INARA.
SIMON ASKED THAT I LOOK AFTER HER, AND RIVER WAS BEING SO KIND AS TO HELP ME PACK--
IF IT'S ALL THE SAME TO YOU, INARA, NOW'S NOT THE TIME TO HAVE THIS CONVERSATION.
AGAIN.
MAL, I'M ONLY TRYING TO SET A SCHEDULE FOR MY DEPARTURE. AND WHILE I CAN, AND HAVE, APPRECIATED THAT YOU HAVE A BUSINESS TO RUN...
I MUST ASK YOU TO REMEMBER THAT I DO AS WELL.
LOOK, INARA, I'M GETTING YOU WHERE YOU WANT TO GO AS FAST AS I CAN. NOW, MAYBE IT'S NOT AS FAST AS YOU'D LIKE, BUT IT'S NOT EXACTLY NEXT DOOR AND I'VE GOT TO TAKE WHAT I CAN ALONG THE WAY. TO BE CLEAR...
...I WILL GET YOU WHERE YOU WANT TO BE, AND UNDERSTAND THAT'S NOT HERE.
MAL...
LET THE BALL OF YARN GO.

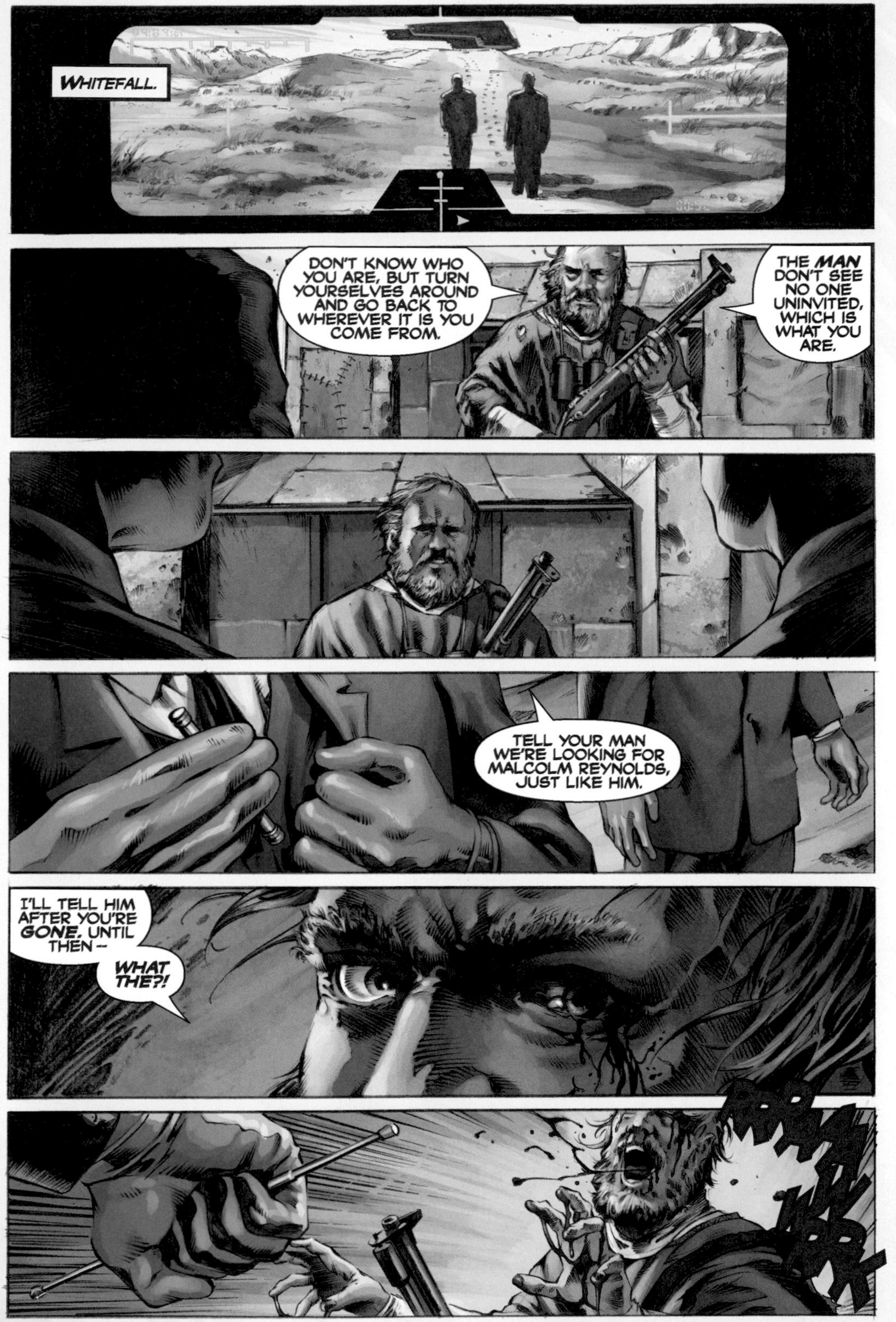
WHITEFALL.
DON'T KNOW WHO YOU ARE, BUT TURN YOURSELVES AROUND AND GO BACK TO WHEREVER IT IS YOU COME FROM.
THE MAN DON'T SEE NO ONE UNINVITED, WHICH IS WHAT YOU ARE.
TELL YOUR MAN WE'RE LOOKING FOR MALCOLM REYNOLDS, JUST LIKE HIM.
I'LL TELL HIM AFTER YOU'RE GONE. UNTIL THEN --
WHAT THE?!

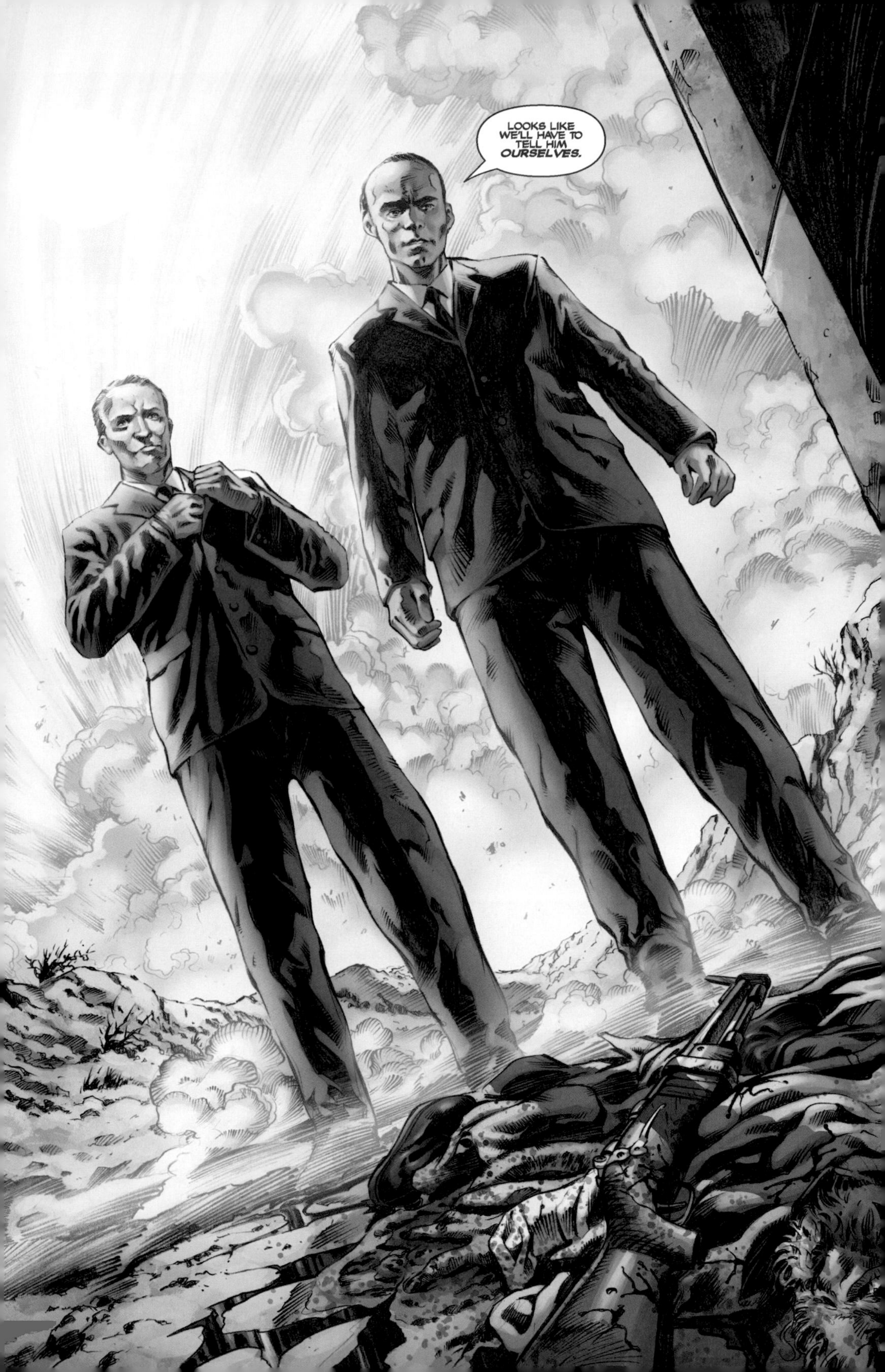
LOOKS LIKE WE'LL HAVE TO TELL HIM *OURSELVES.*

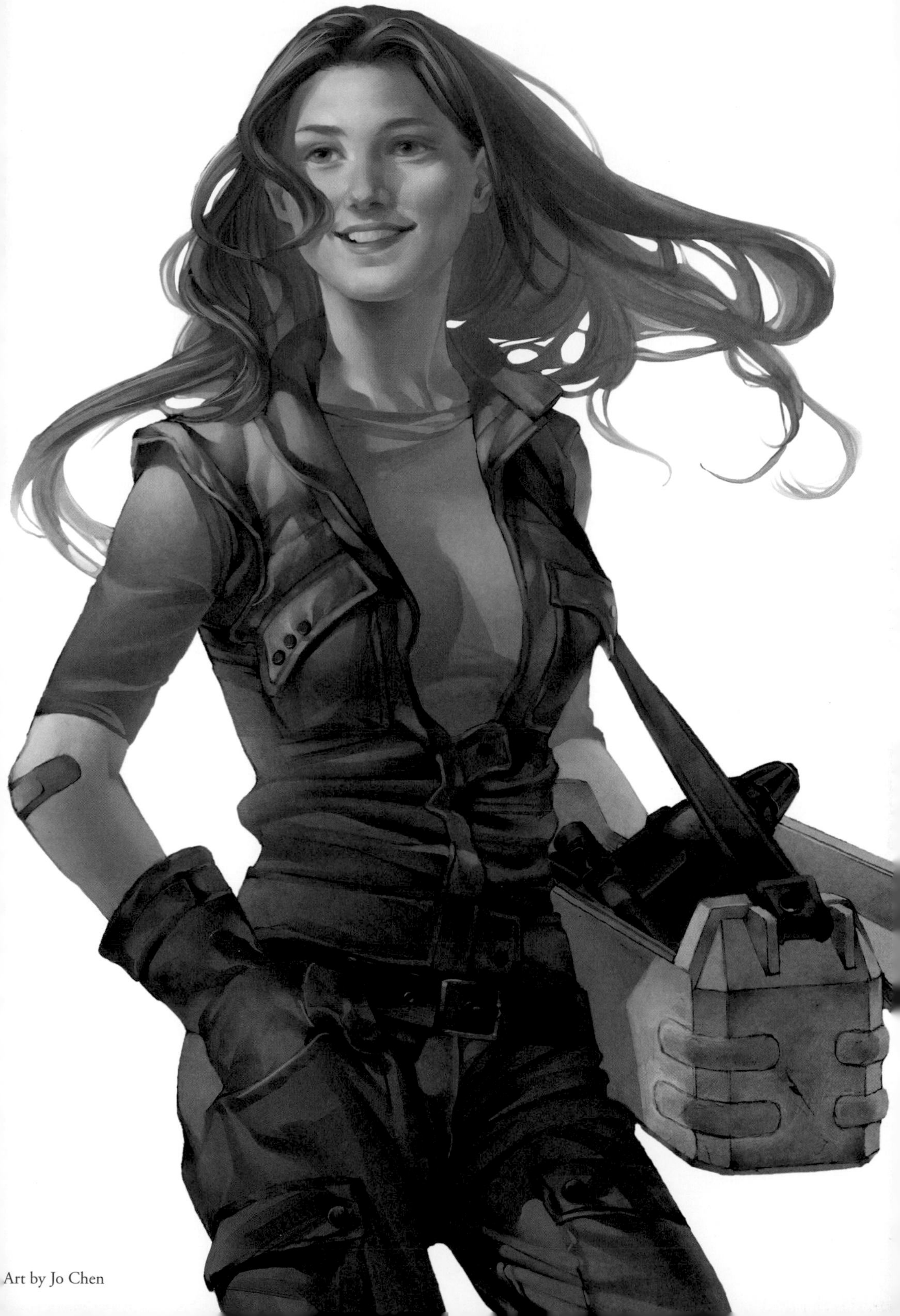

Art by Jo Chen

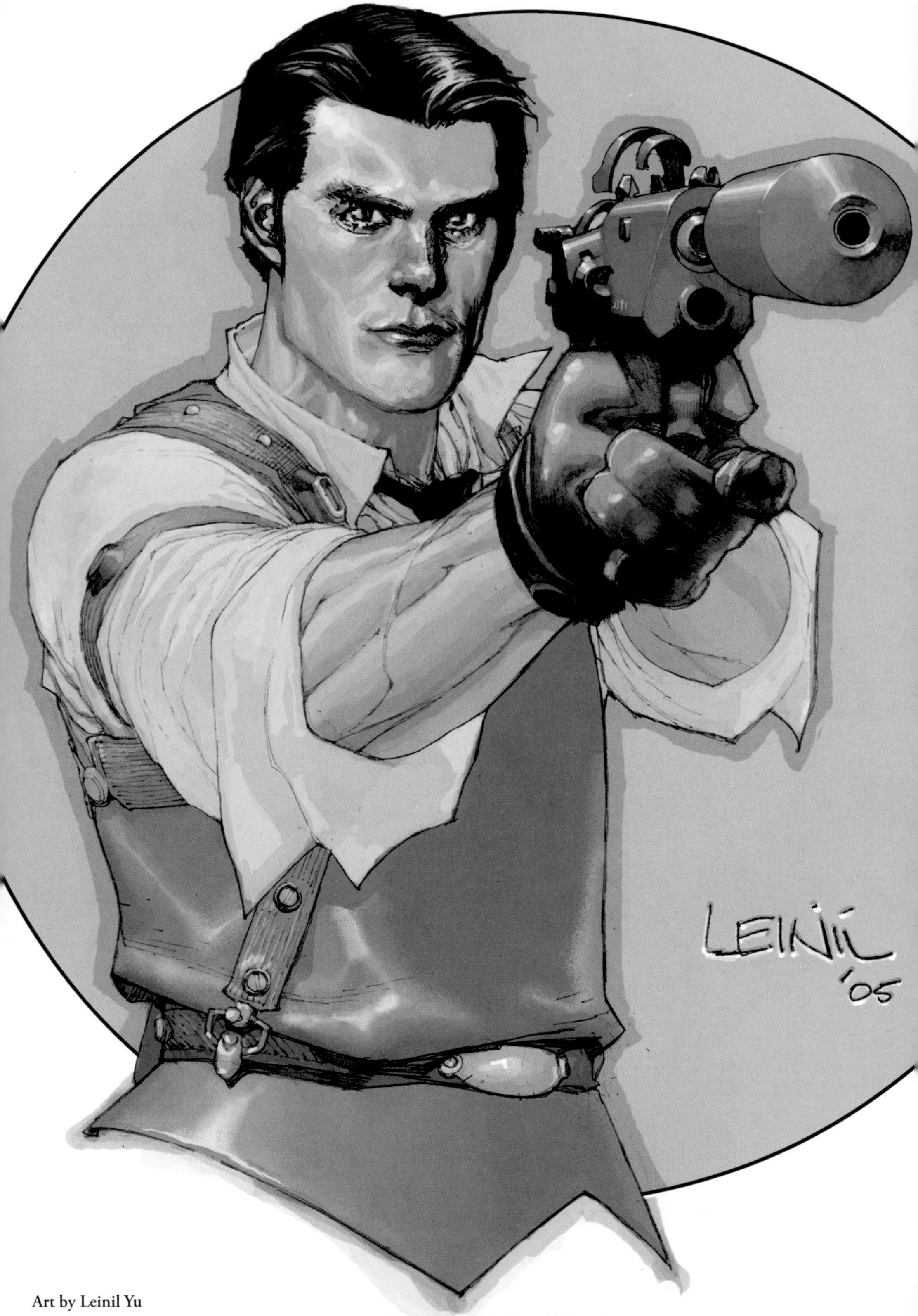
LEINIL
'05

Art by Leinil Yu

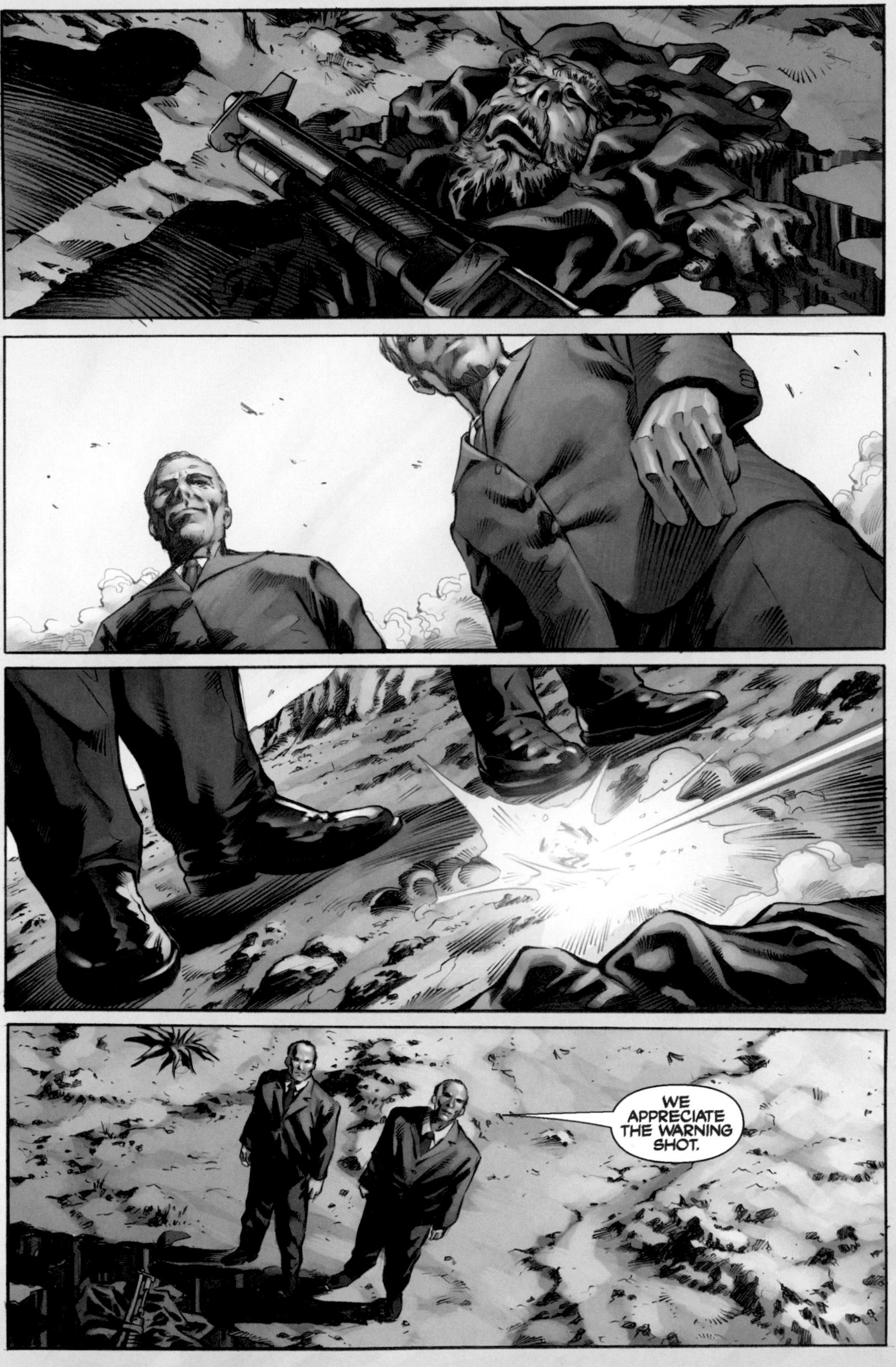
WE APPRECIATE THE WARNING SHOT.

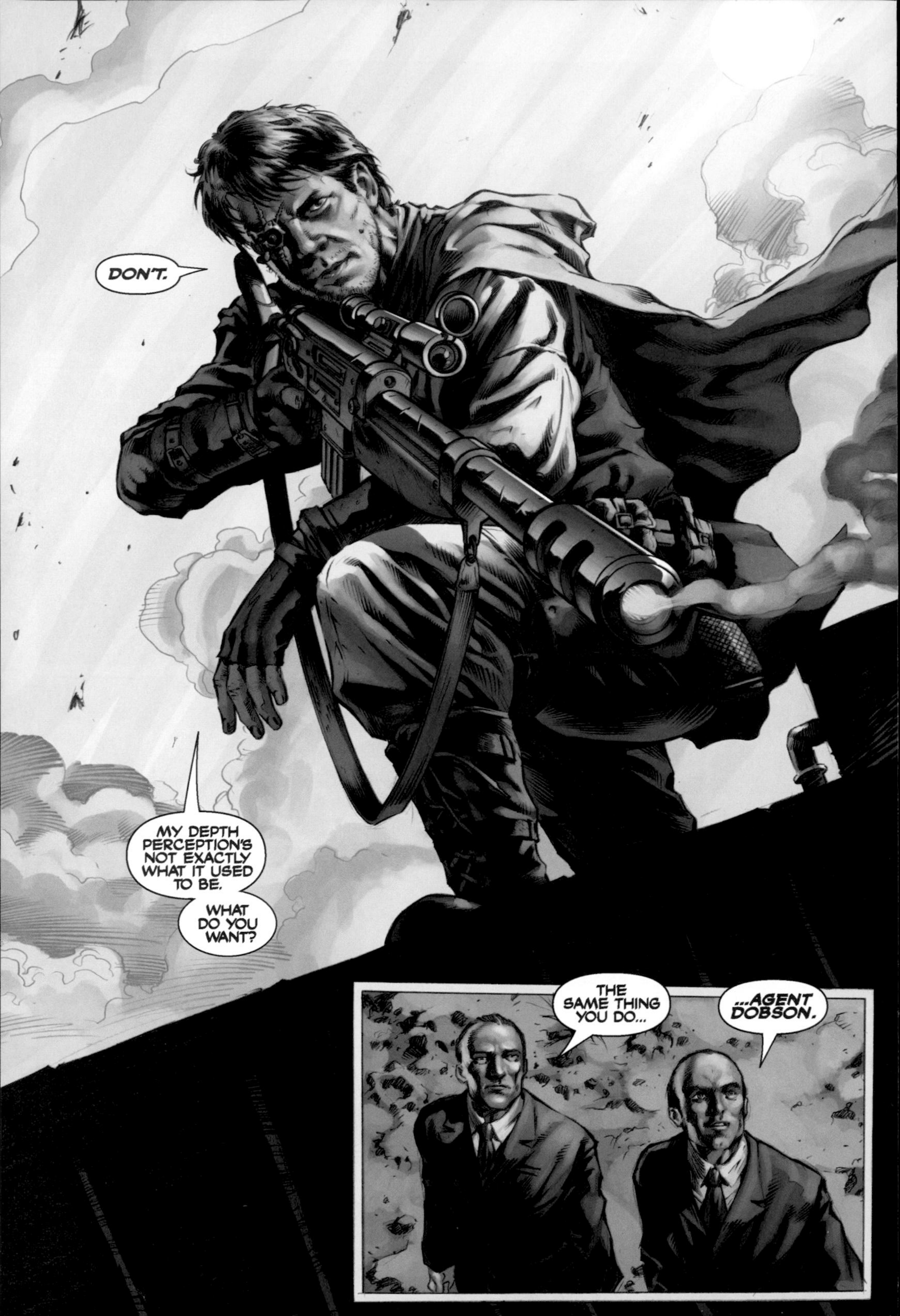
DON'T.
MY DEPTH PERCEPTION'S NOT EXACTLY WHAT IT USED TO BE.
WHAT DO YOU WANT?
THE SAME THING YOU DO...
...AGENT DOBSON.

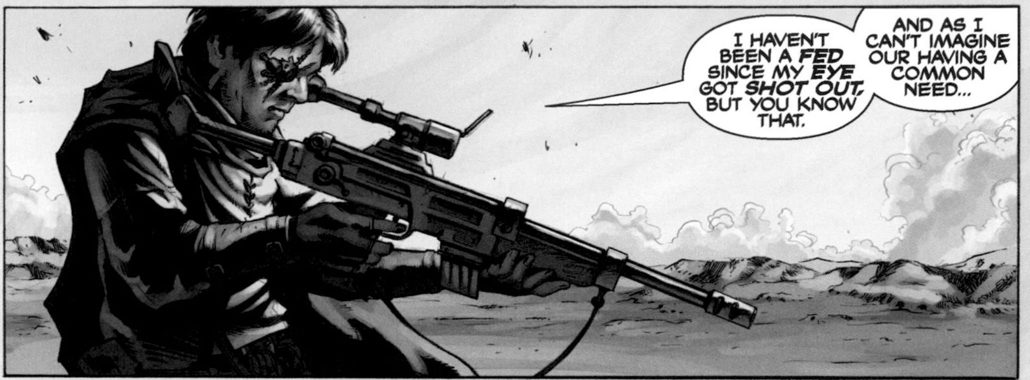
I HAVEN'T BEEN A FED SINCE MY EYE GOT SHOT OUT, BUT YOU KNOW THAT.
AND AS I CAN'T IMAGINE OUR HAVING A COMMON NEED...

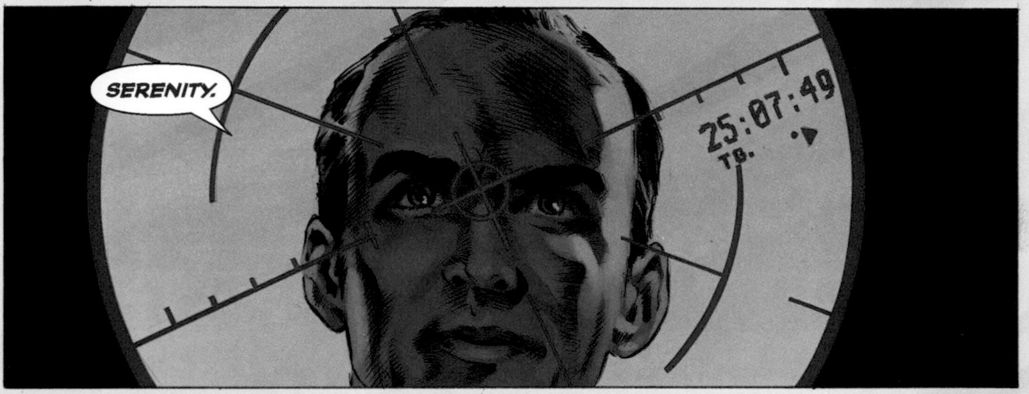
SERENITY.
25:07:49
TB.

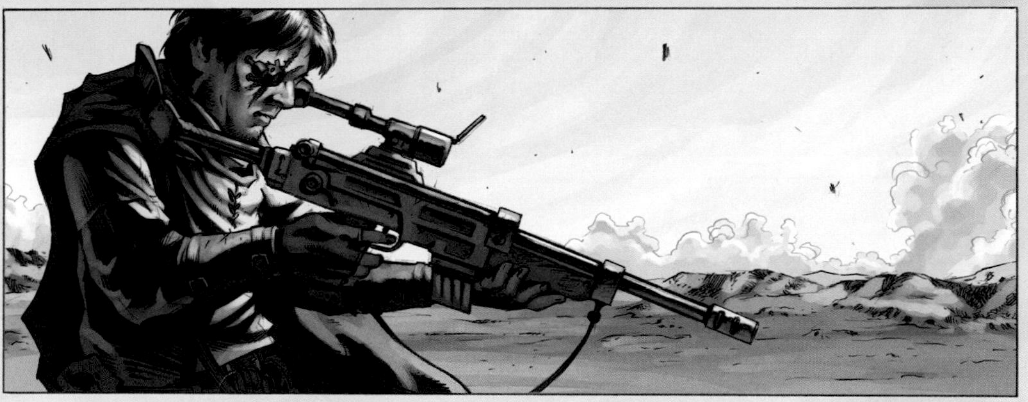

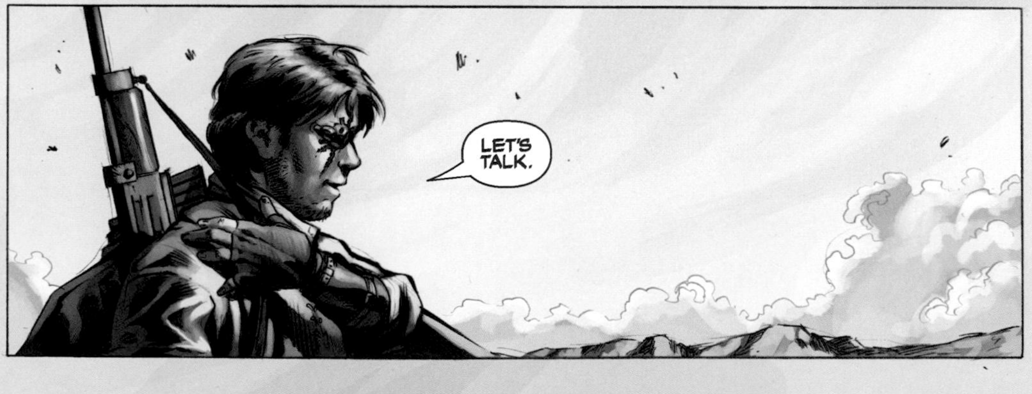
LET'S TALK.

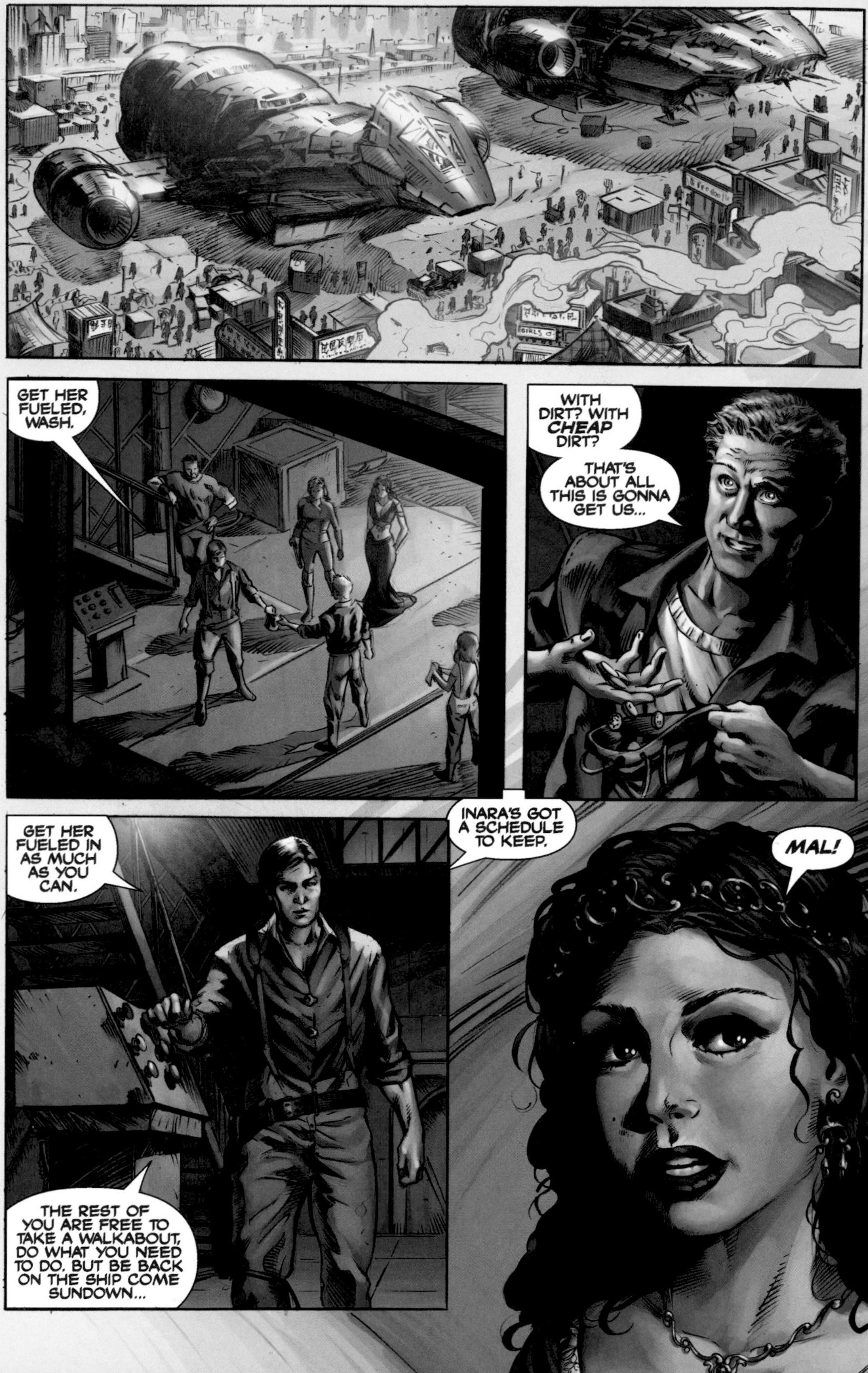
GET HER FUELED, WASH.
WITH DIRT? WITH *CHEAP* DIRT?
THAT'S ABOUT ALL THIS IS GONNA GET US...
GET HER FUELED IN AS MUCH AS YOU CAN.
INARA'S GOT A SCHEDULE TO KEEP.
THE REST OF YOU ARE FREE TO TAKE A WALKABOUT, DO WHAT YOU NEED TO DO. BUT BE BACK ON THE SHIP COME SUNDOWN...
MAL!

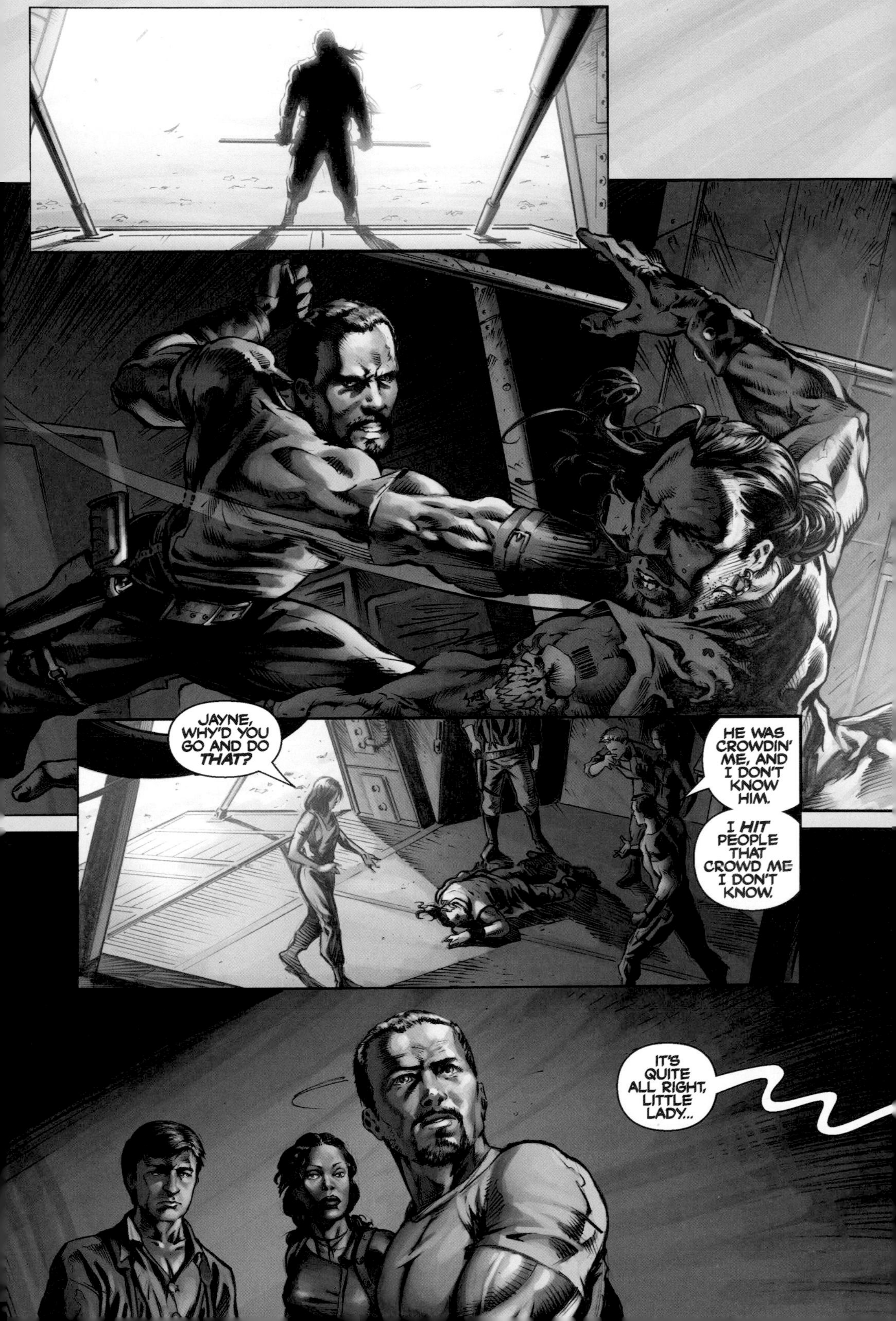
JAYNE, WHY'D YOU GO AND DO *THAT?*
HE WAS CROWDIN' ME, AND I DON'T KNOW HIM.
I *HIT* PEOPLE THAT CROWD ME I DON'T KNOW.
IT'S QUITE ALL RIGHT, LITTLE LADY...

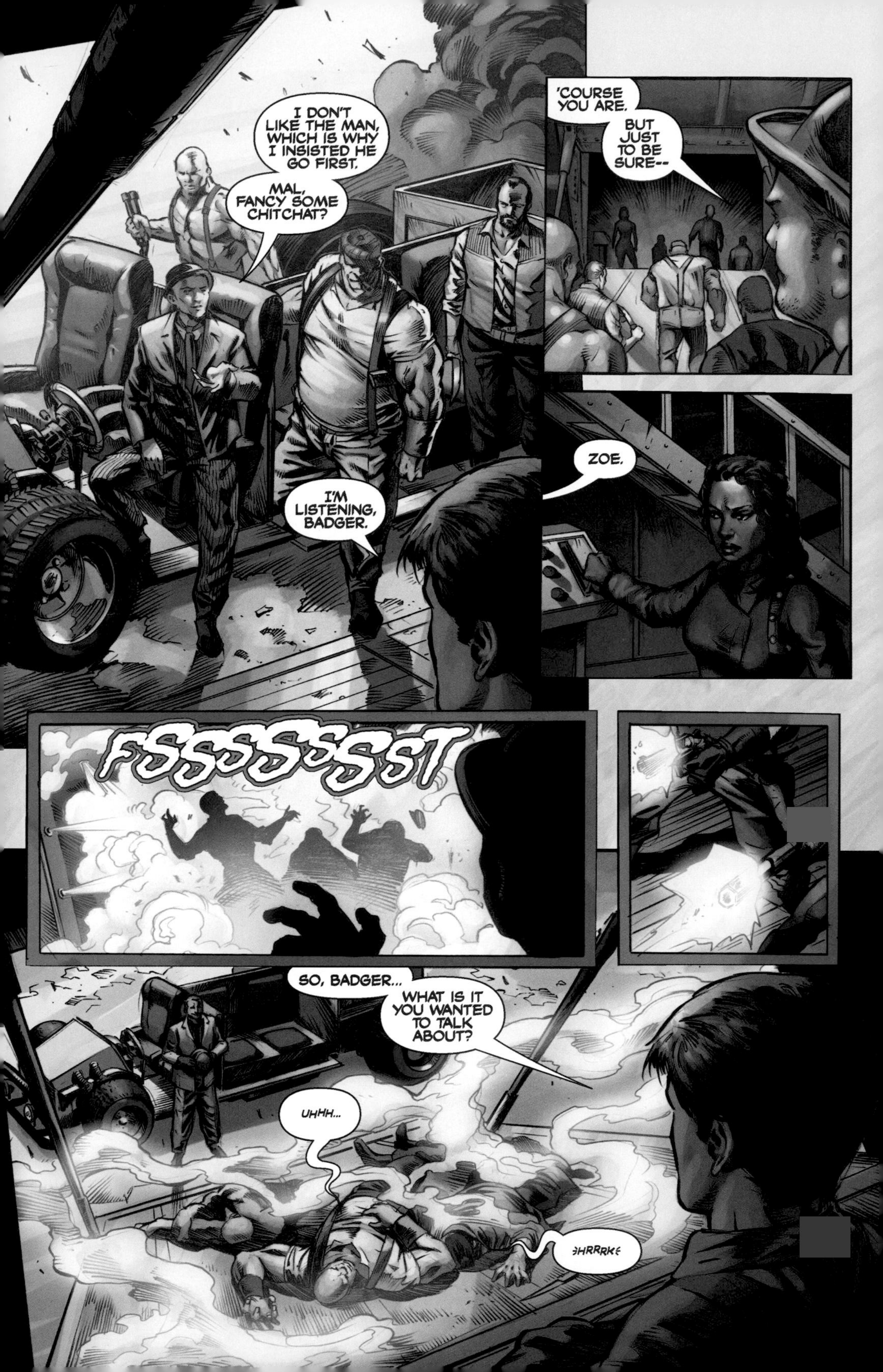
I DON'T LIKE THE MAN, WHICH IS WHY I INSISTED HE GO FIRST.
MAL, FANCY SOME CHITCHAT?
I'M LISTENING, BADGER.
'COURSE YOU ARE.
BUT JUST TO BE SURE--
ZOE.
FSSSSSSST
SO, BADGER...
WHAT IS IT YOU WANTED TO TALK ABOUT?
UHHH...
HRRRK

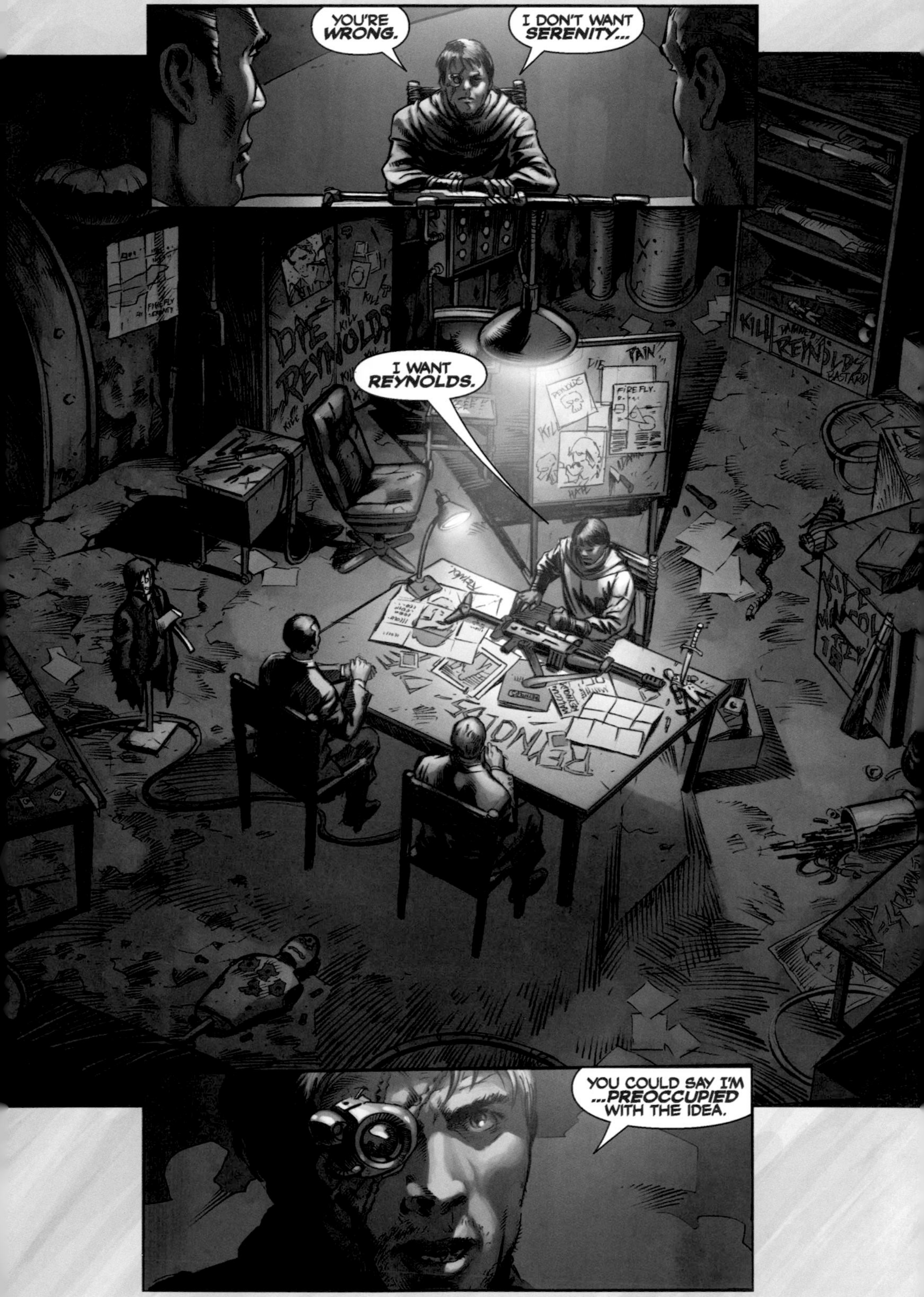
YOU'RE WRONG.
I DON'T WANT SERENITY...
I WANT REYNOLDS.
DIE REYNOLDS
KILL
FIREFLY
PAIN
REYNOLDS
YOU COULD SAY I'M ...PREOCCUPIED WITH THE IDEA.

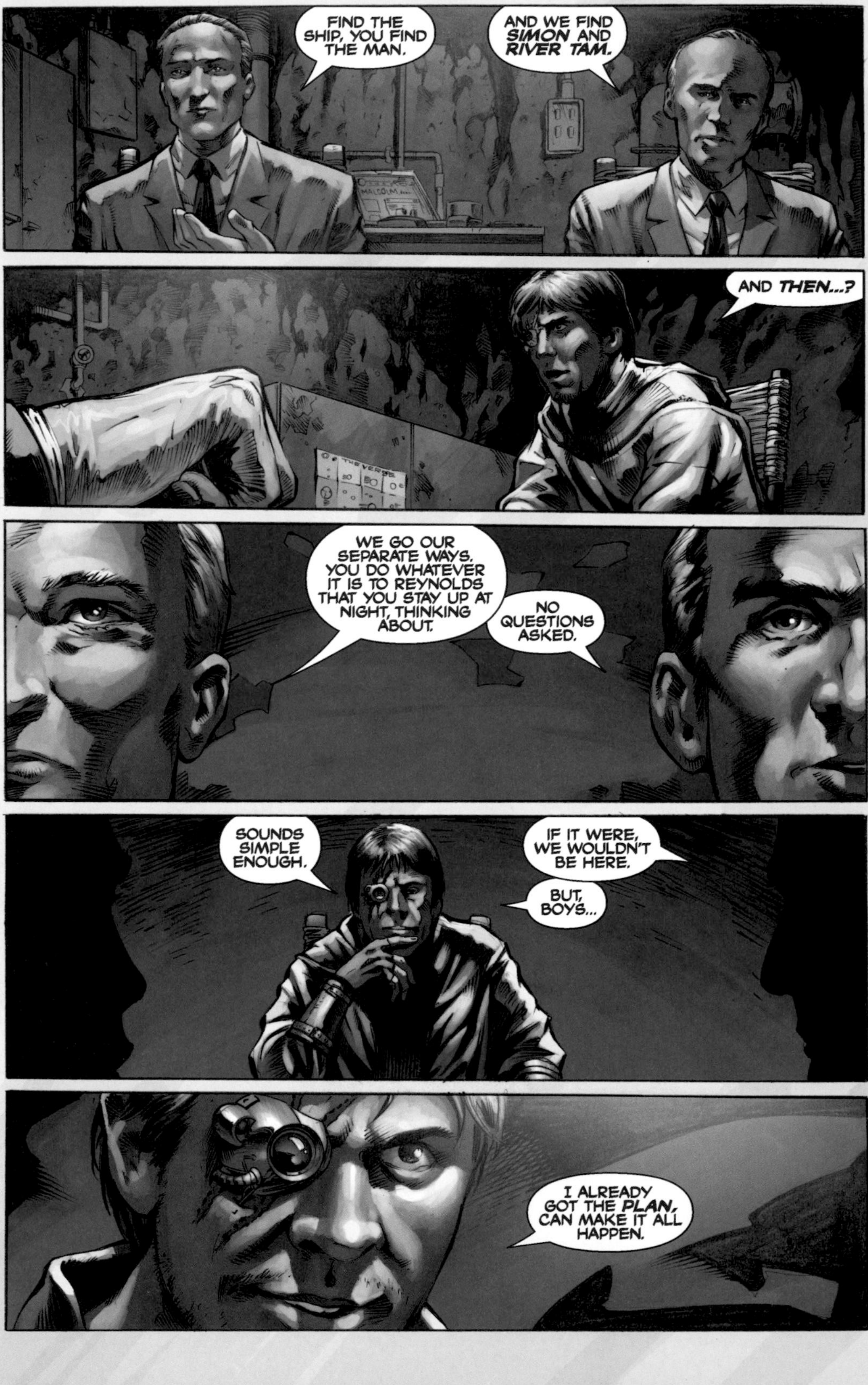
FIND THE SHIP, YOU FIND THE MAN.
AND WE FIND *SIMON* AND *RIVER TAM.*
MALCOLM...
AND *THEN...?*
THE VERSE
WE GO OUR SEPARATE WAYS. YOU DO WHATEVER IT IS TO REYNOLDS THAT YOU STAY UP AT NIGHT, THINKING ABOUT.
NO QUESTIONS ASKED.
SOUNDS SIMPLE ENOUGH.
IF IT WERE, WE WOULDN'T BE HERE.
BUT, BOYS...
I ALREADY GOT THE *PLAN*, CAN MAKE IT ALL HAPPEN.

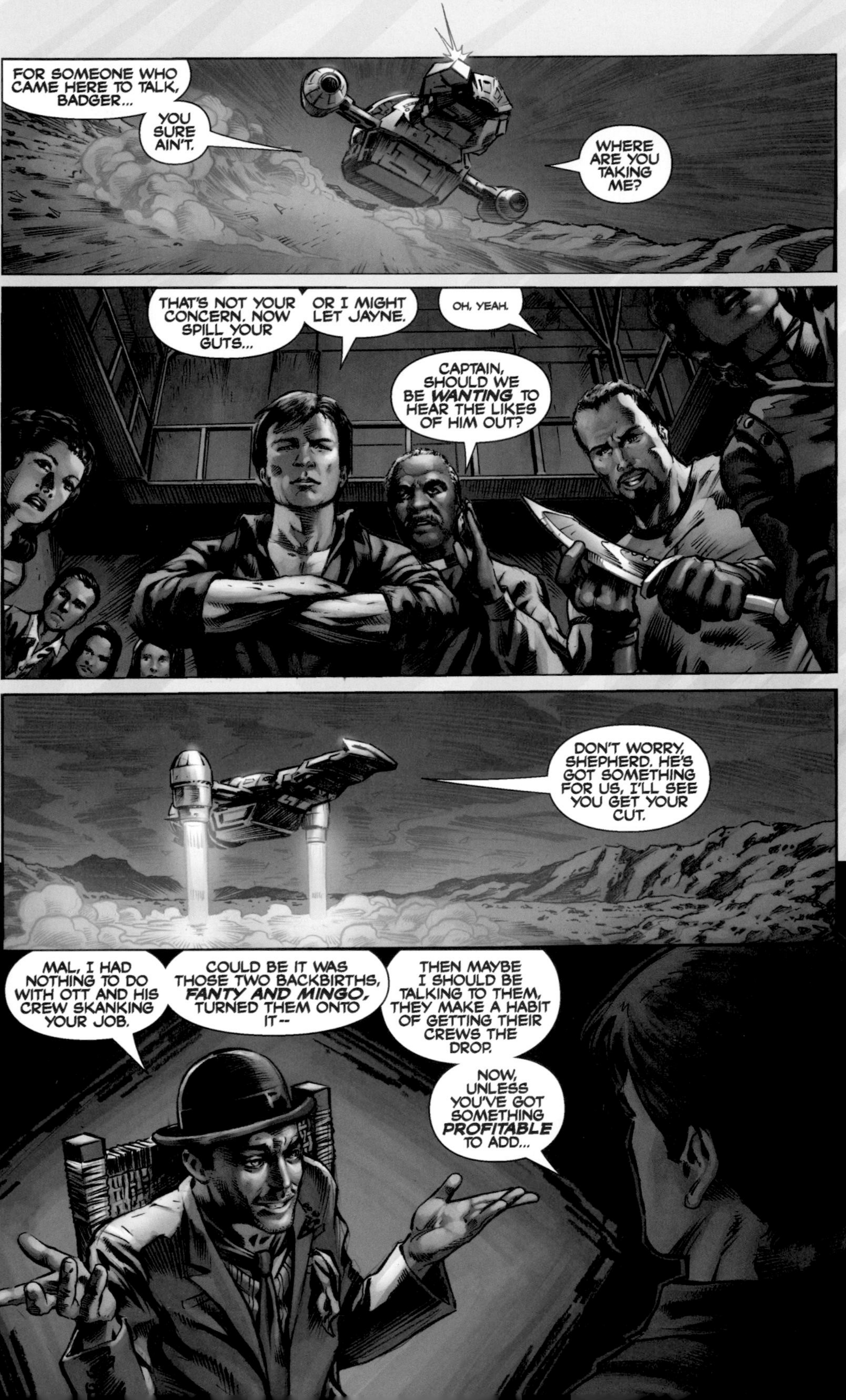
FOR SOMEONE WHO CAME HERE TO TALK, BADGER...
YOU SURE AIN'T.
WHERE ARE YOU TAKING ME?
THAT'S NOT YOUR CONCERN. NOW SPILL YOUR GUTS...
OR I MIGHT LET JAYNE.
OH, YEAH.
CAPTAIN, SHOULD WE BE WANTING TO HEAR THE LIKES OF HIM OUT?
DON'T WORRY, SHEPHERD. HE'S GOT SOMETHING FOR US, I'LL SEE YOU GET YOUR CUT.
MAL, I HAD NOTHING TO DO WITH OTT AND HIS CREW SKANKING YOUR JOB.
COULD BE IT WAS THOSE TWO BACKBIRTHS, FANTY AND MINGO, TURNED THEM ONTO IT--
THEN MAYBE I SHOULD BE TALKING TO THEM, THEY MAKE A HABIT OF GETTING THEIR CREWS THE DROP.
NOW, UNLESS YOU'VE GOT SOMETHING PROFITABLE TO ADD...

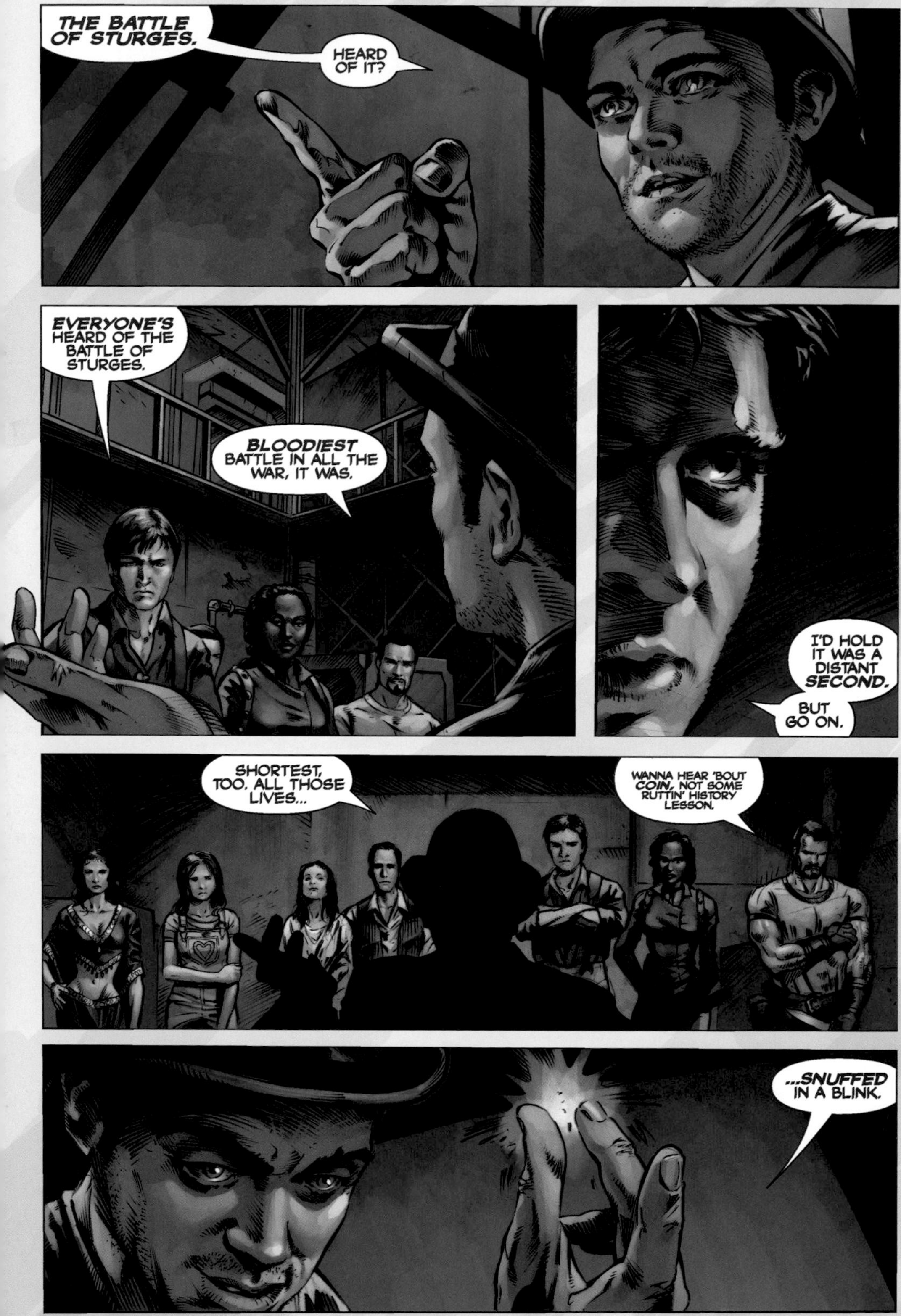

THE BATTLE OF STURGES.
HEARD OF IT?
EVERYONE'S HEARD OF THE BATTLE OF STURGES.
BLOODIEST BATTLE IN ALL THE WAR, IT WAS.
I'D HOLD IT WAS A DISTANT SECOND.
BUT GO ON.
SHORTEST, TOO. ALL THOSE LIVES...
WANNA HEAR 'BOUT COIN, NOT SOME RUTTIN' HISTORY LESSON.
...SNUFFED IN A BLINK.

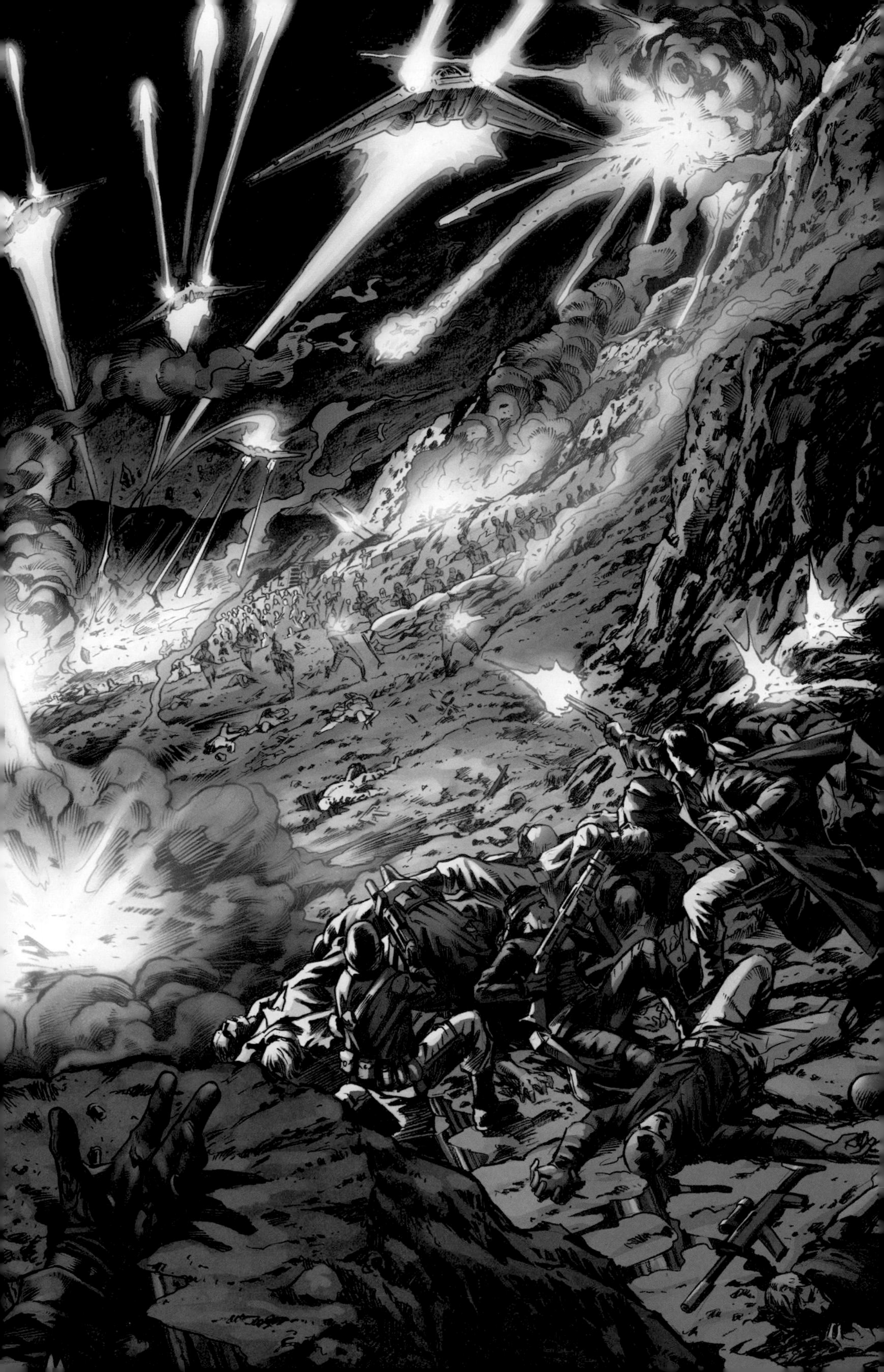

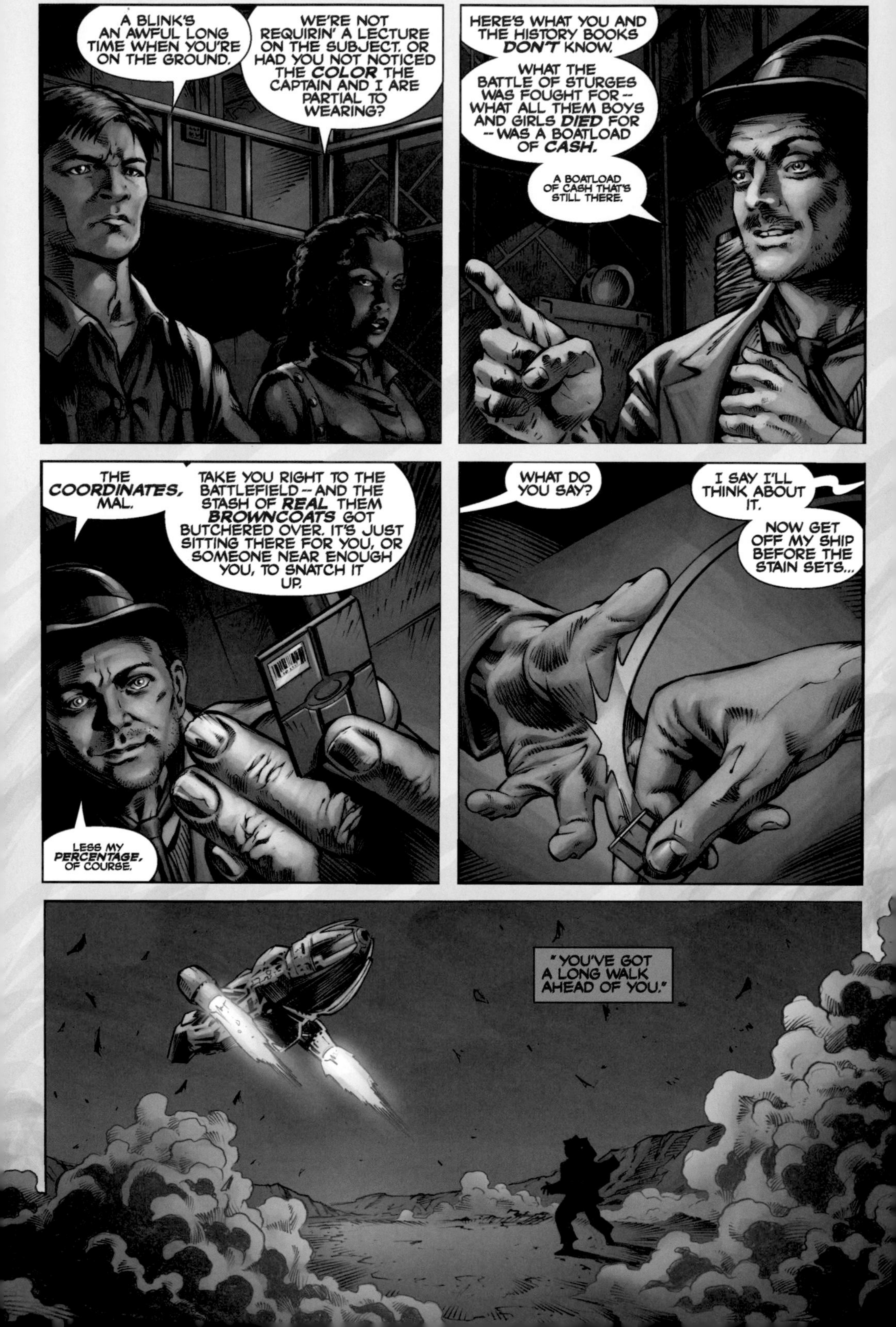
A BLINK'S AN AWFUL LONG TIME WHEN YOU'RE ON THE GROUND.
WE'RE NOT REQUIRIN' A LECTURE ON THE SUBJECT. OR HAD YOU NOT NOTICED THE COLOR THE CAPTAIN AND I ARE PARTIAL TO WEARING?
HERE'S WHAT YOU AND THE HISTORY BOOKS DON'T KNOW.
WHAT THE BATTLE OF STURGES WAS FOUGHT FOR -- WHAT ALL THEM BOYS AND GIRLS DIED FOR -- WAS A BOATLOAD OF CASH.
A BOATLOAD OF CASH THAT'S STILL THERE.
THE COORDINATES, MAL.
TAKE YOU RIGHT TO THE BATTLEFIELD -- AND THE STASH OF REAL THEM BROWNCOATS GOT BUTCHERED OVER. IT'S JUST SITTING THERE FOR YOU, OR SOMEONE NEAR ENOUGH YOU, TO SNATCH IT UP.
LESS MY PERCENTAGE, OF COURSE.
WHAT DO YOU SAY?
I SAY I'LL THINK ABOUT IT.
NOW GET OFF MY SHIP BEFORE THE STAIN SETS...
"YOU'VE GOT A LONG WALK AHEAD OF YOU."

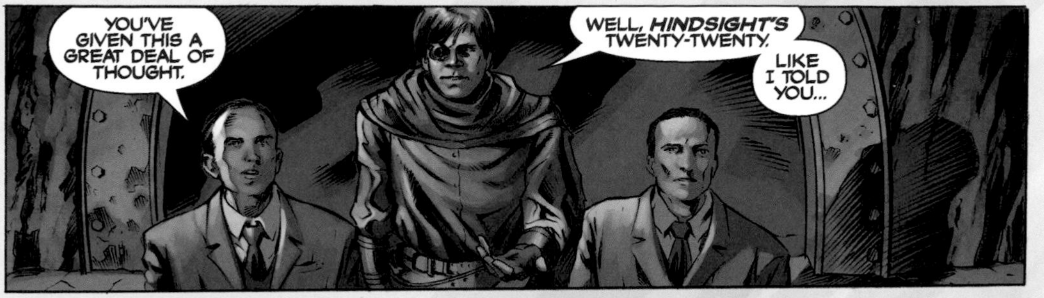
YOU'VE GIVEN THIS A GREAT DEAL OF THOUGHT.
WELL, HINDSIGHT'S TWENTY-TWENTY.
LIKE I TOLD YOU...

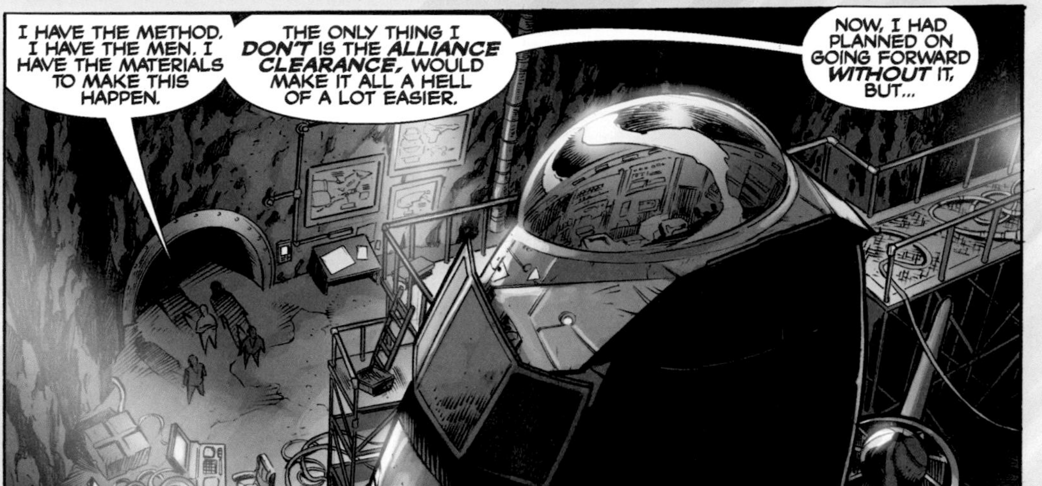
I HAVE THE METHOD. I HAVE THE MEN. I HAVE THE MATERIALS TO MAKE THIS HAPPEN.
THE ONLY THING I DON'T IS THE ALLIANCE CLEARANCE, WOULD MAKE IT ALL A HELL OF A LOT EASIER.
NOW, I HAD PLANNED ON GOING FORWARD WITHOUT IT, BUT...

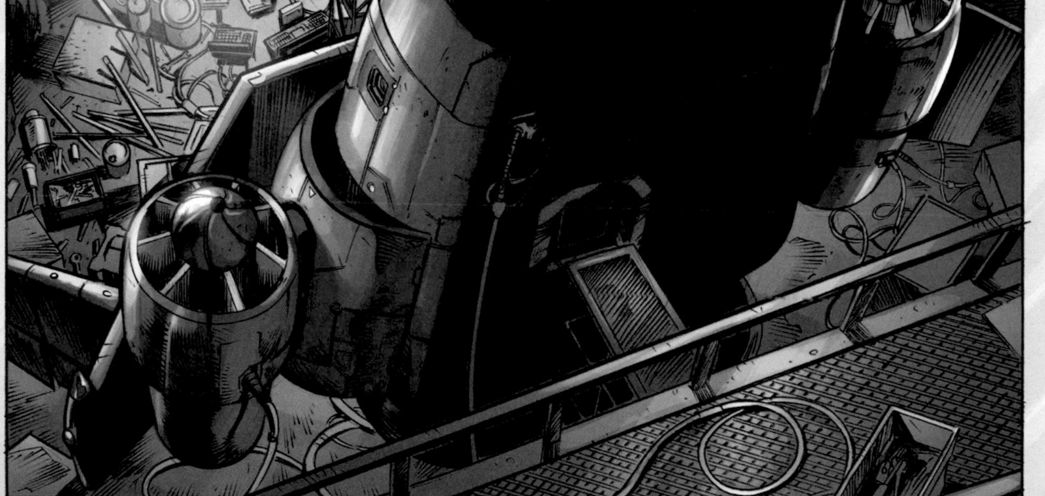
YOU NEED SAY NO MORE, MR. DOBSON.

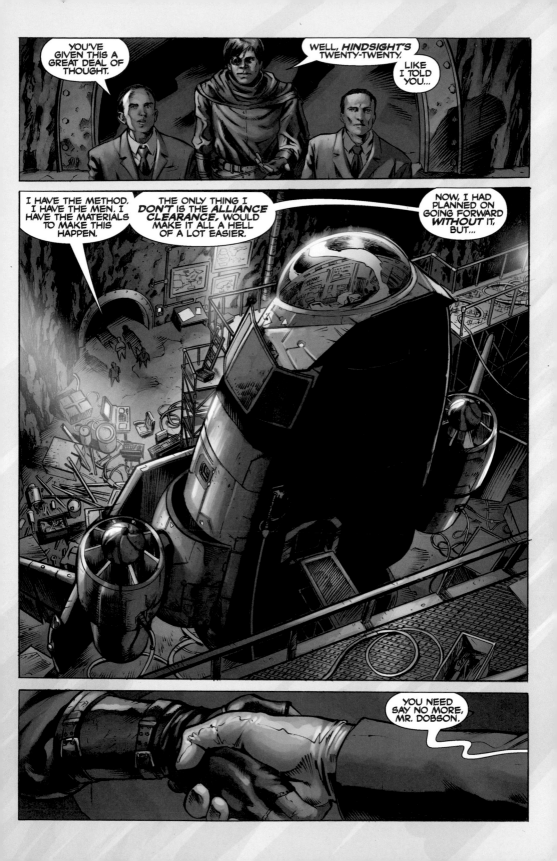

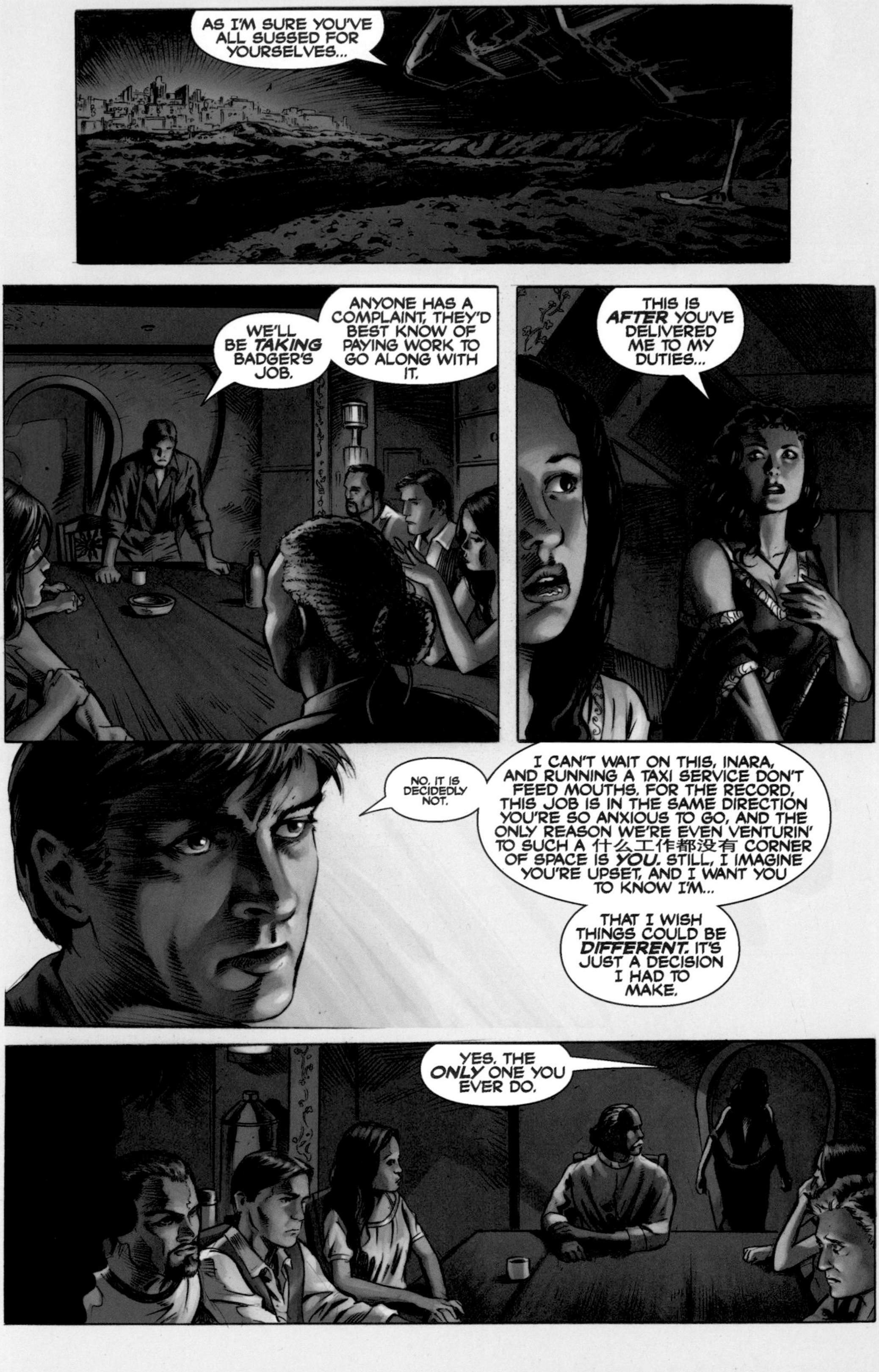
AS I'M SURE YOU'VE ALL SUSSED FOR YOURSELVES...
WE'LL BE TAKING BADGER'S JOB.
ANYONE HAS A COMPLAINT, THEY'D BEST KNOW OF PAYING WORK TO GO ALONG WITH IT.
THIS IS AFTER YOU'VE DELIVERED ME TO MY DUTIES...
NO, IT IS DECIDEDLY NOT.
I CAN'T WAIT ON THIS, INARA, AND RUNNING A TAXI SERVICE DON'T FEED MOUTHS. FOR THE RECORD, THIS JOB IS IN THE SAME DIRECTION YOU'RE SO ANXIOUS TO GO, AND THE ONLY REASON WE'RE EVEN VENTURIN' TO SUCH A 什么工作都没有 CORNER OF SPACE IS YOU. STILL, I IMAGINE YOU'RE UPSET, AND I WANT YOU TO KNOW I'M...
THAT I WISH THINGS COULD BE DIFFERENT. IT'S JUST A DECISION I HAD TO MAKE.
YES, THE ONLY ONE YOU EVER DO.

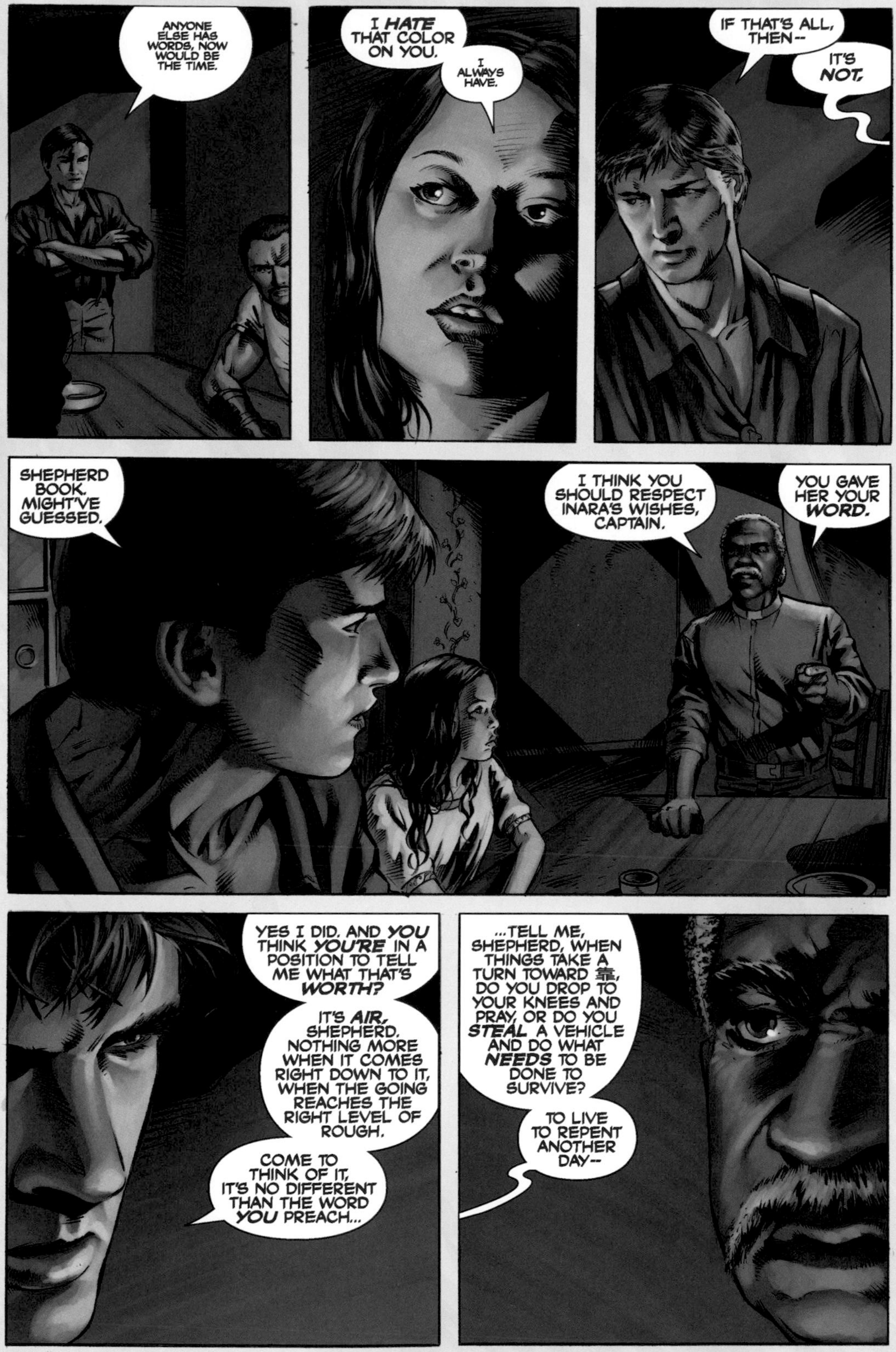
ANYONE ELSE HAS WORDS, NOW WOULD BE THE TIME.
I HATE THAT COLOR ON YOU.
I ALWAYS HAVE.
IF THAT'S ALL, THEN--
IT'S NOT.
SHEPHERD BOOK. MIGHT'VE GUESSED.
I THINK YOU SHOULD RESPECT INARA'S WISHES, CAPTAIN.
YOU GAVE HER YOUR WORD.
YES I DID. AND YOU THINK YOU'RE IN A POSITION TO TELL ME WHAT THAT'S WORTH?
IT'S AIR, SHEPHERD. NOTHING MORE WHEN IT COMES RIGHT DOWN TO IT, WHEN THE GOING REACHES THE RIGHT LEVEL OF ROUGH.
COME TO THINK OF IT, IT'S NO DIFFERENT THAN THE WORD YOU PREACH...
...TELL ME, SHEPHERD, WHEN THINGS TAKE A TURN TOWARD 靠, DO YOU DROP TO YOUR KNEES AND PRAY, OR DO YOU STEAL A VEHICLE AND DO WHAT NEEDS TO BE DONE TO SURVIVE?
TO LIVE TO REPENT ANOTHER DAY--

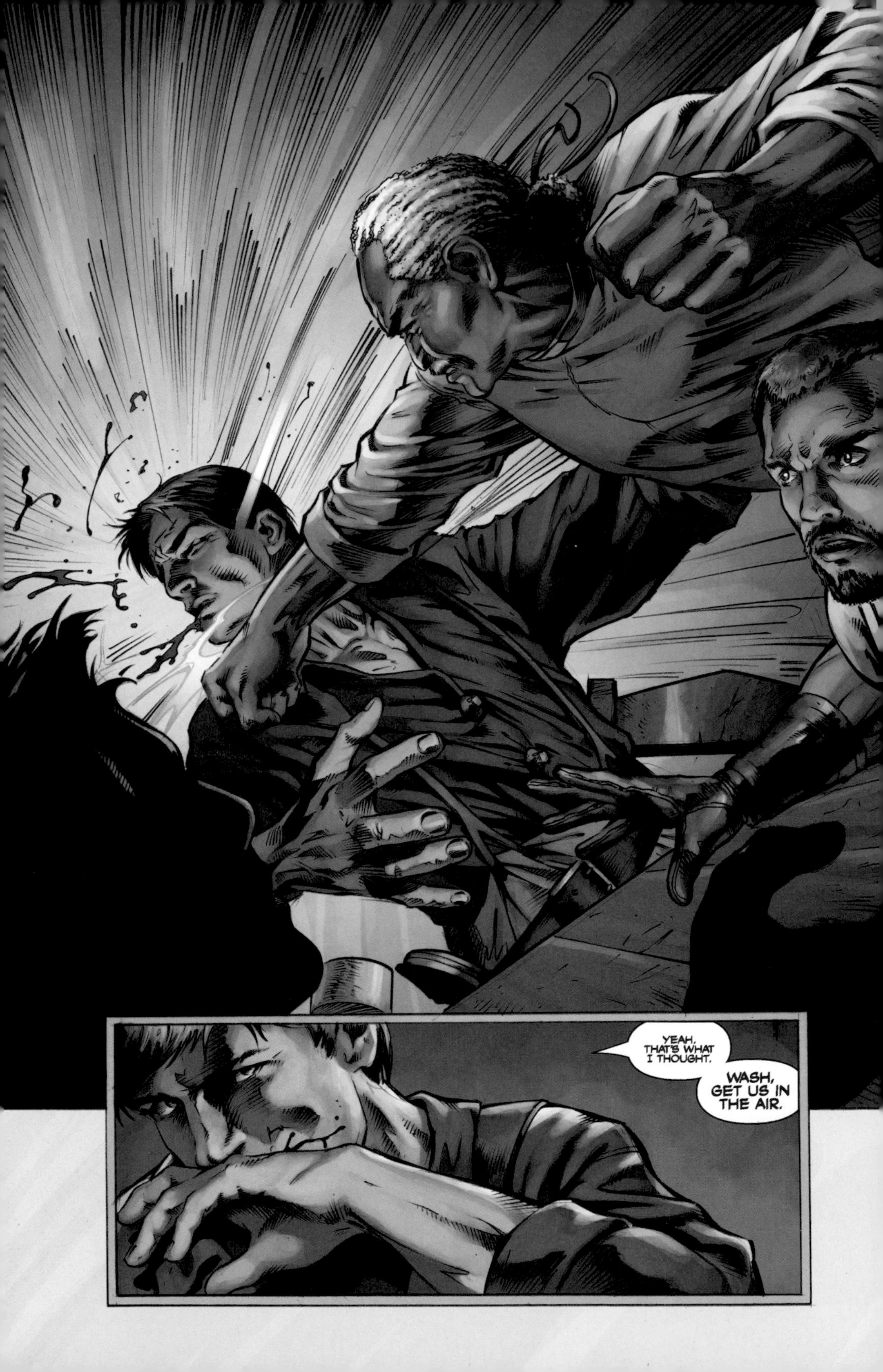
YEAH, THAT'S WHAT I THOUGHT.
WASH, GET US IN THE AIR.

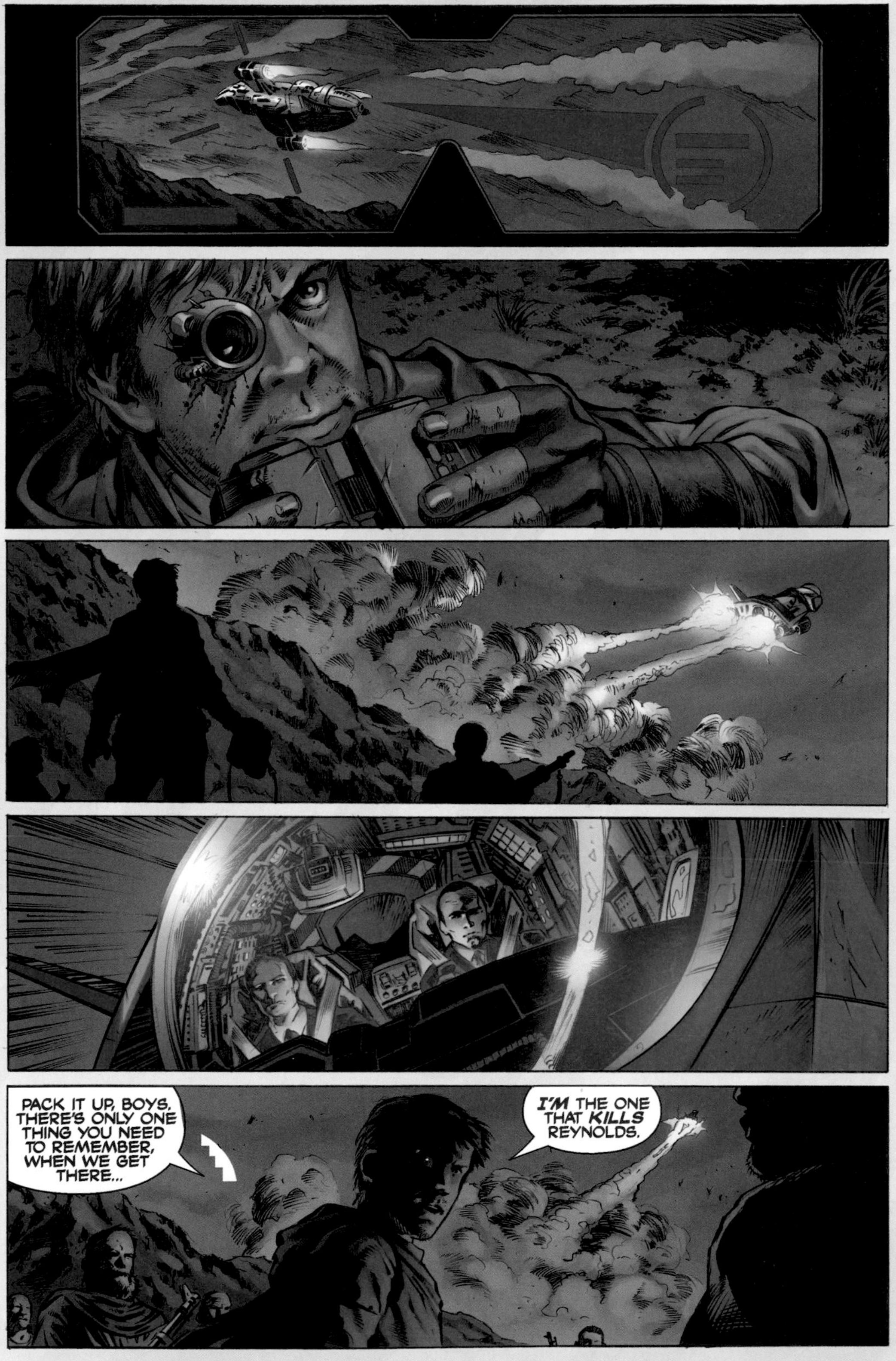
PACK IT UP, BOYS. THERE'S ONLY ONE THING YOU NEED TO REMEMBER, WHEN WE GET THERE...
I'M THE ONE THAT KILLS REYNOLDS.

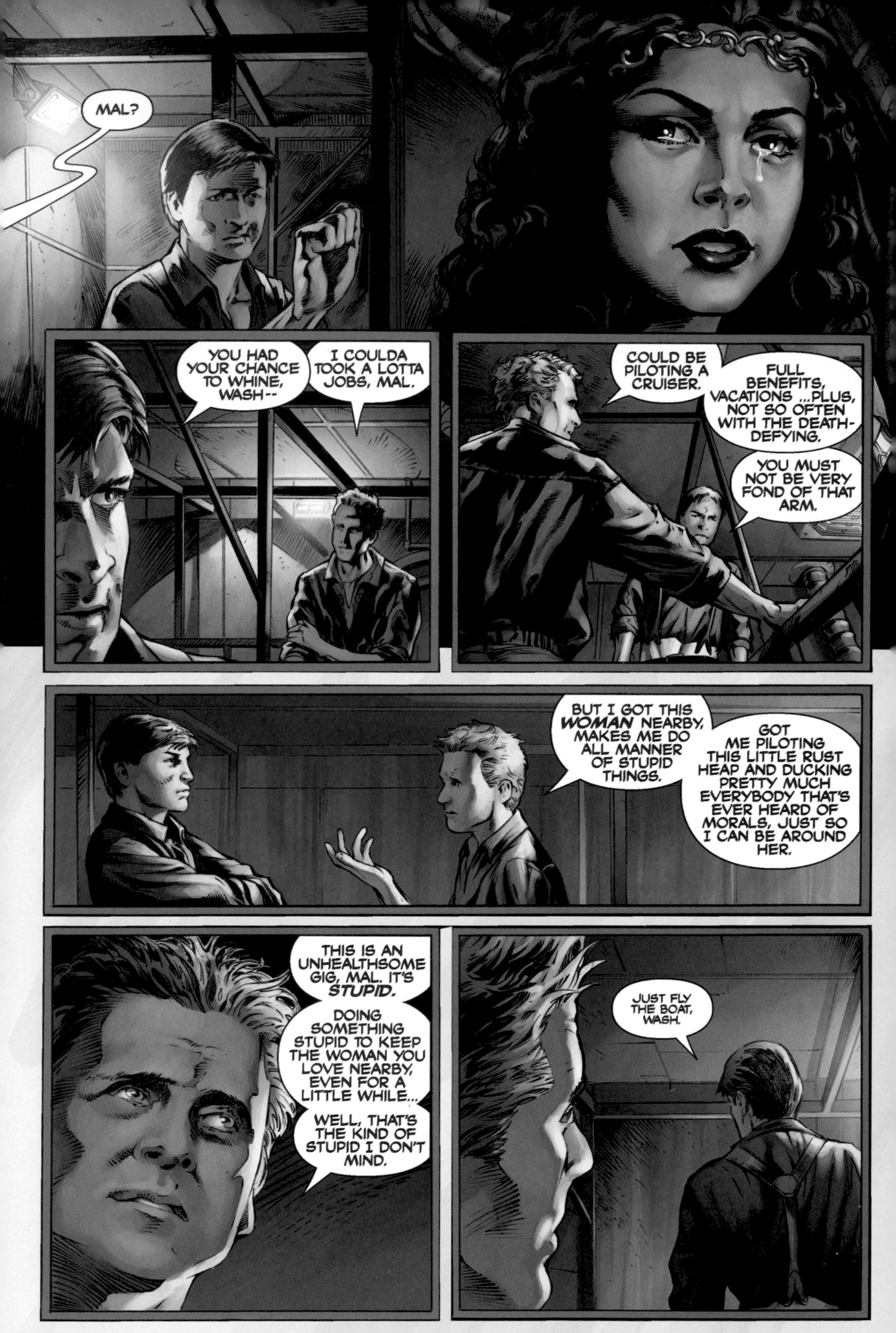
MAL?
YOU HAD YOUR CHANCE TO WHINE, WASH--
I COULDA TOOK A LOTTA JOBS, MAL.
COULD BE PILOTING A CRUISER.
FULL BENEFITS, VACATIONS ...PLUS, NOT SO OFTEN WITH THE DEATH-DEFYING.
YOU MUST NOT BE VERY FOND OF THAT ARM.
BUT I GOT THIS WOMAN NEARBY, MAKES ME DO ALL MANNER OF STUPID THINGS.
GOT ME PILOTING THIS LITTLE RUST HEAP AND DUCKING PRETTY MUCH EVERYBODY THAT'S EVER HEARD OF MORALS, JUST SO I CAN BE AROUND HER.
THIS IS AN UNHEALTHSOME GIG, MAL. IT'S STUPID.
DOING SOMETHING STUPID TO KEEP THE WOMAN YOU LOVE NEARBY, EVEN FOR A LITTLE WHILE...
WELL, THAT'S THE KIND OF STUPID I DON'T MIND.
JUST FLY THE BOAT, WASH.

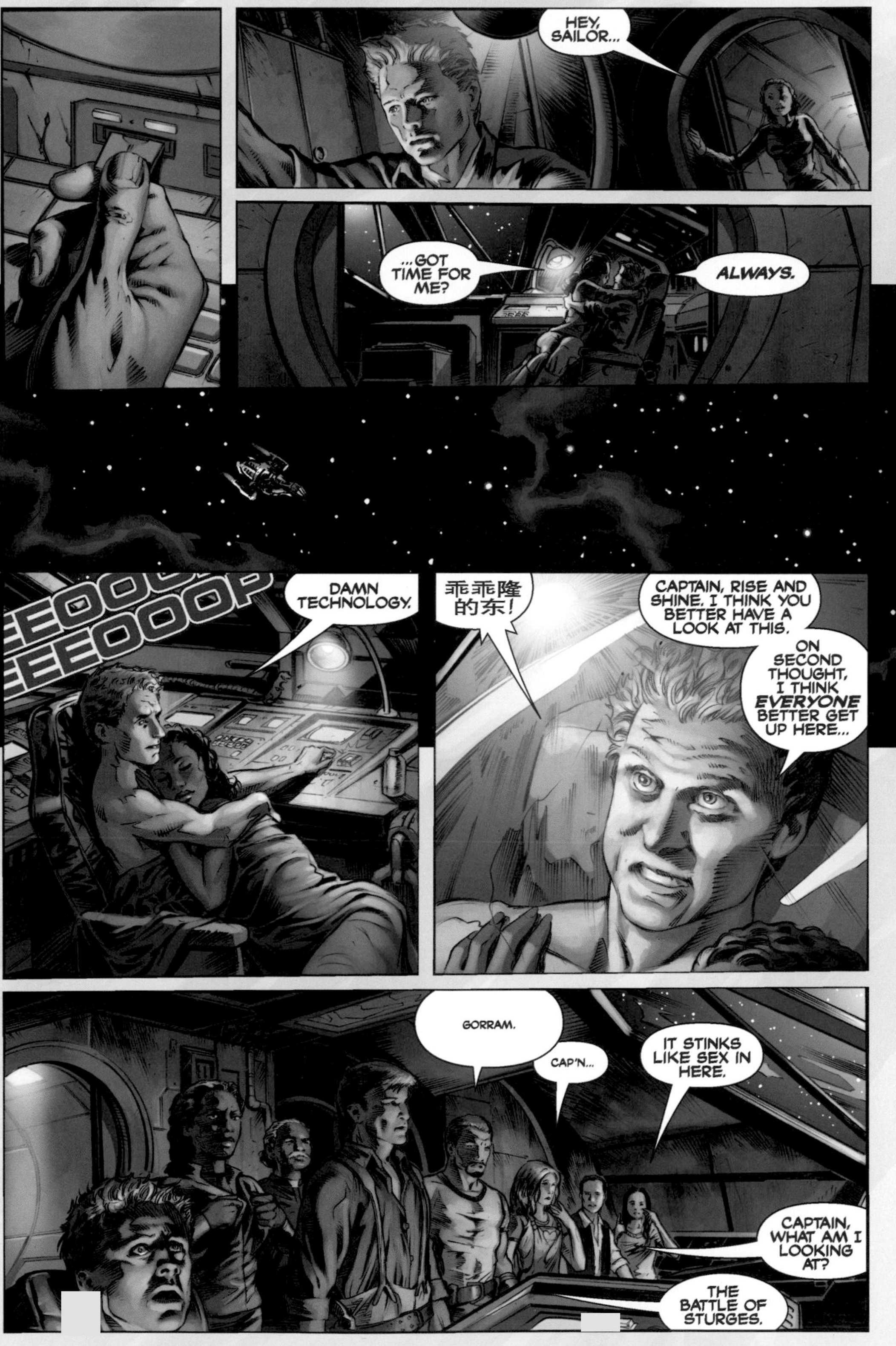
HEY, SAILOR...
...GOT TIME FOR ME?
ALWAYS.
EEEOOOOP
EEEOOOOP
DAMN TECHNOLOGY.
乖乖隆的东!
CAPTAIN, RISE AND SHINE. I THINK YOU BETTER HAVE A LOOK AT THIS.
ON SECOND THOUGHT, I THINK EVERYONE BETTER GET UP HERE...
GORRAM.
CAP'N...
IT STINKS LIKE SEX IN HERE.
CAPTAIN, WHAT AM I LOOKING AT?
THE BATTLE OF STURGES.

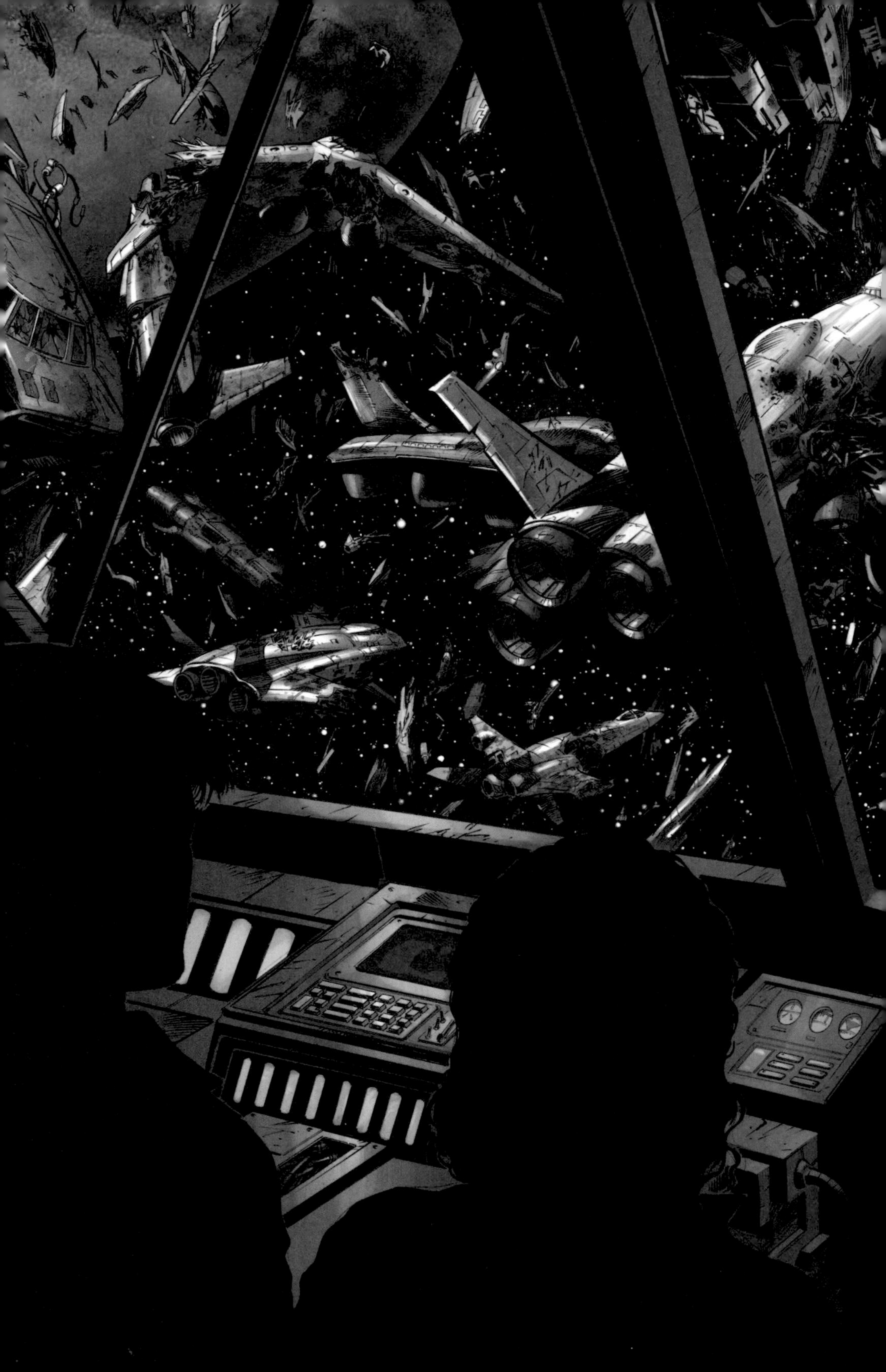

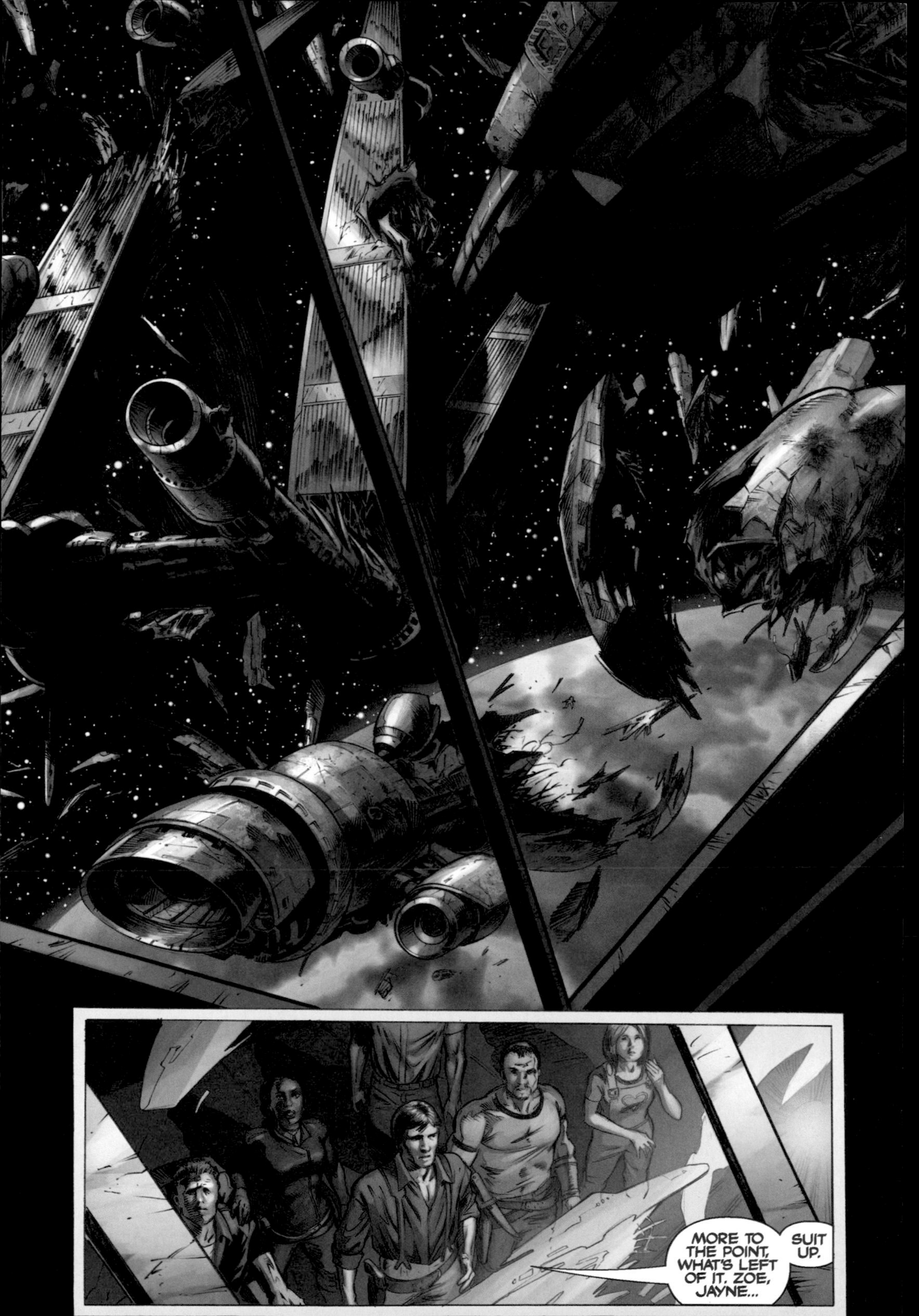
MORE TO THE POINT, WHAT'S LEFT OF IT. ZOE, JAYNE...
SUIT UP.

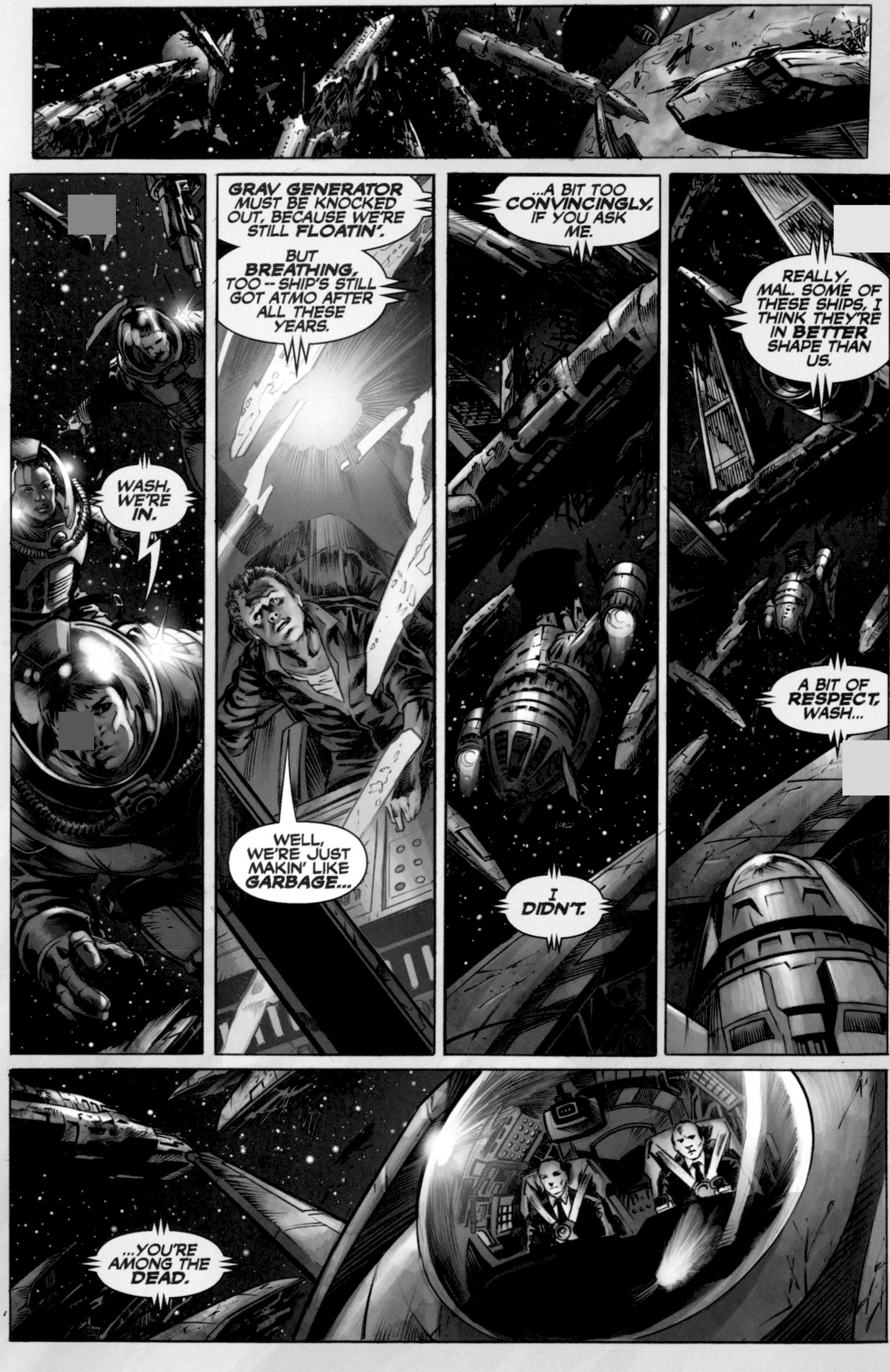
WASH, WE'RE IN.
GRAV GENERATOR MUST BE KNOCKED OUT, BECAUSE WE'RE STILL FLOATIN'.
BUT BREATHING, TOO -- SHIP'S STILL GOT ATMO AFTER ALL THESE YEARS.
WELL, WE'RE JUST MAKIN' LIKE GARBAGE...
...A BIT TOO CONVINCINGLY, IF YOU ASK ME.
I DIDN'T.
REALLY, MAL. SOME OF THESE SHIPS, I THINK THEY'RE IN BETTER SHAPE THAN US.
A BIT OF RESPECT, WASH...
...YOU'RE AMONG THE DEAD.

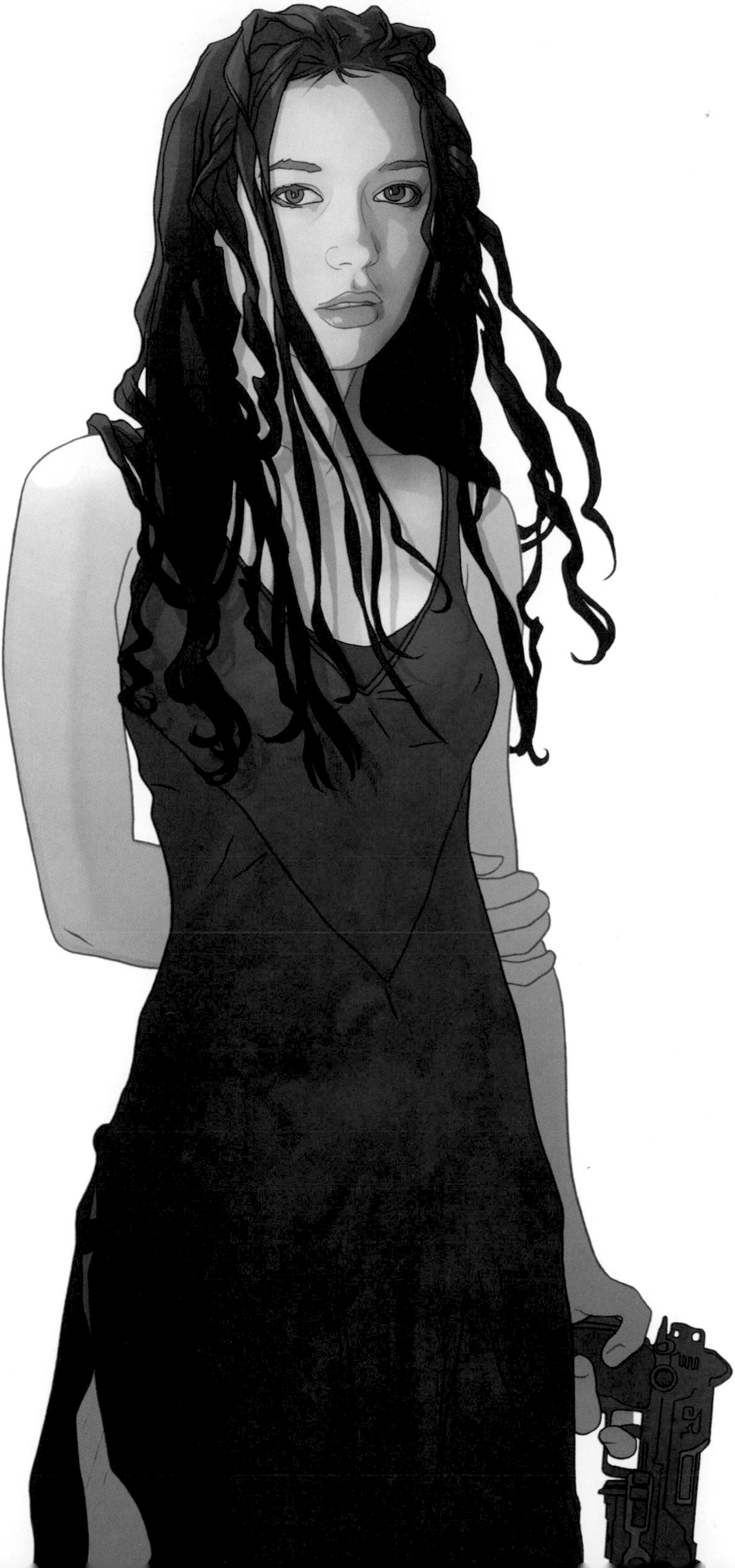

Art by Josh Middleton

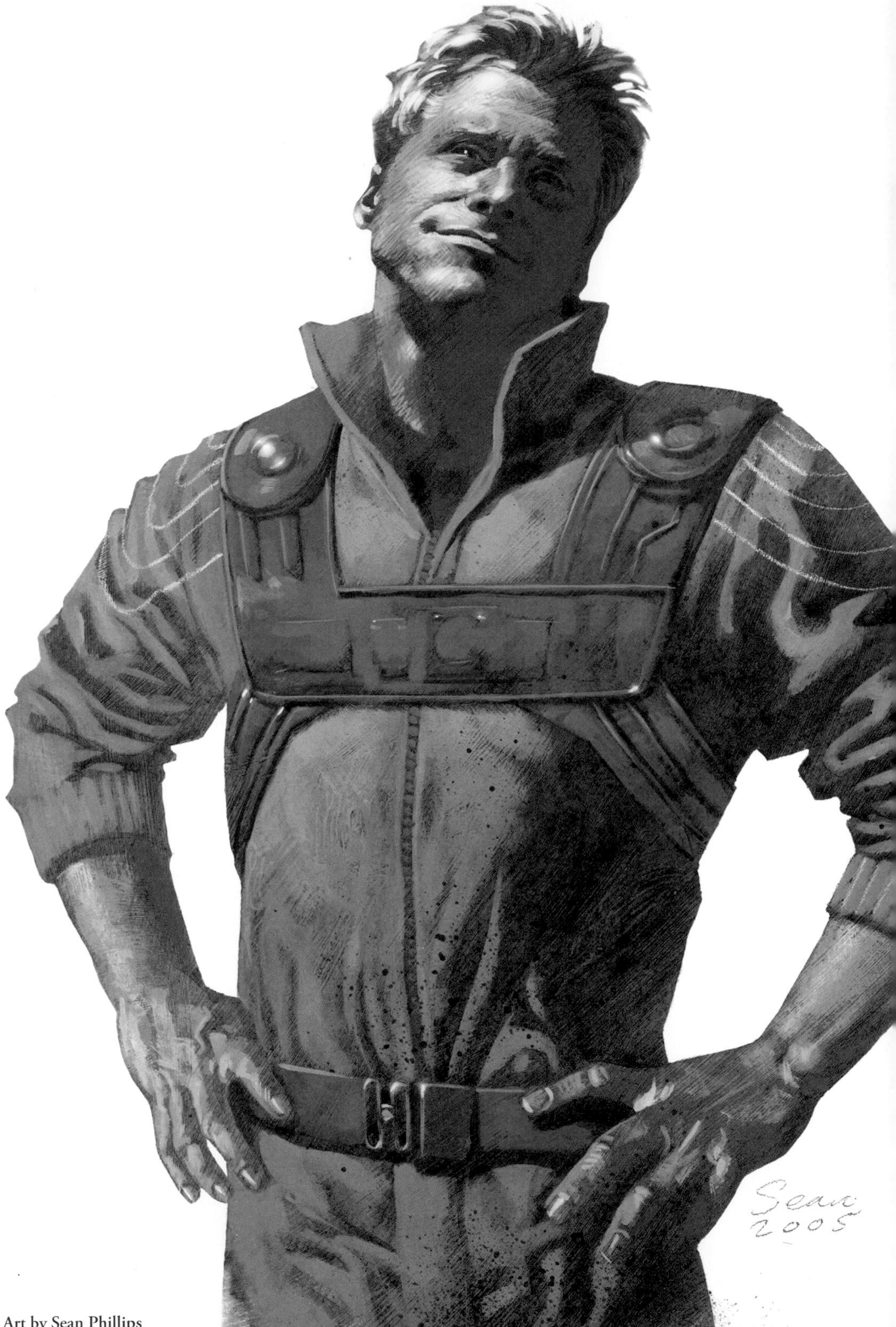
Sean
2005

Art by Sean Phillips

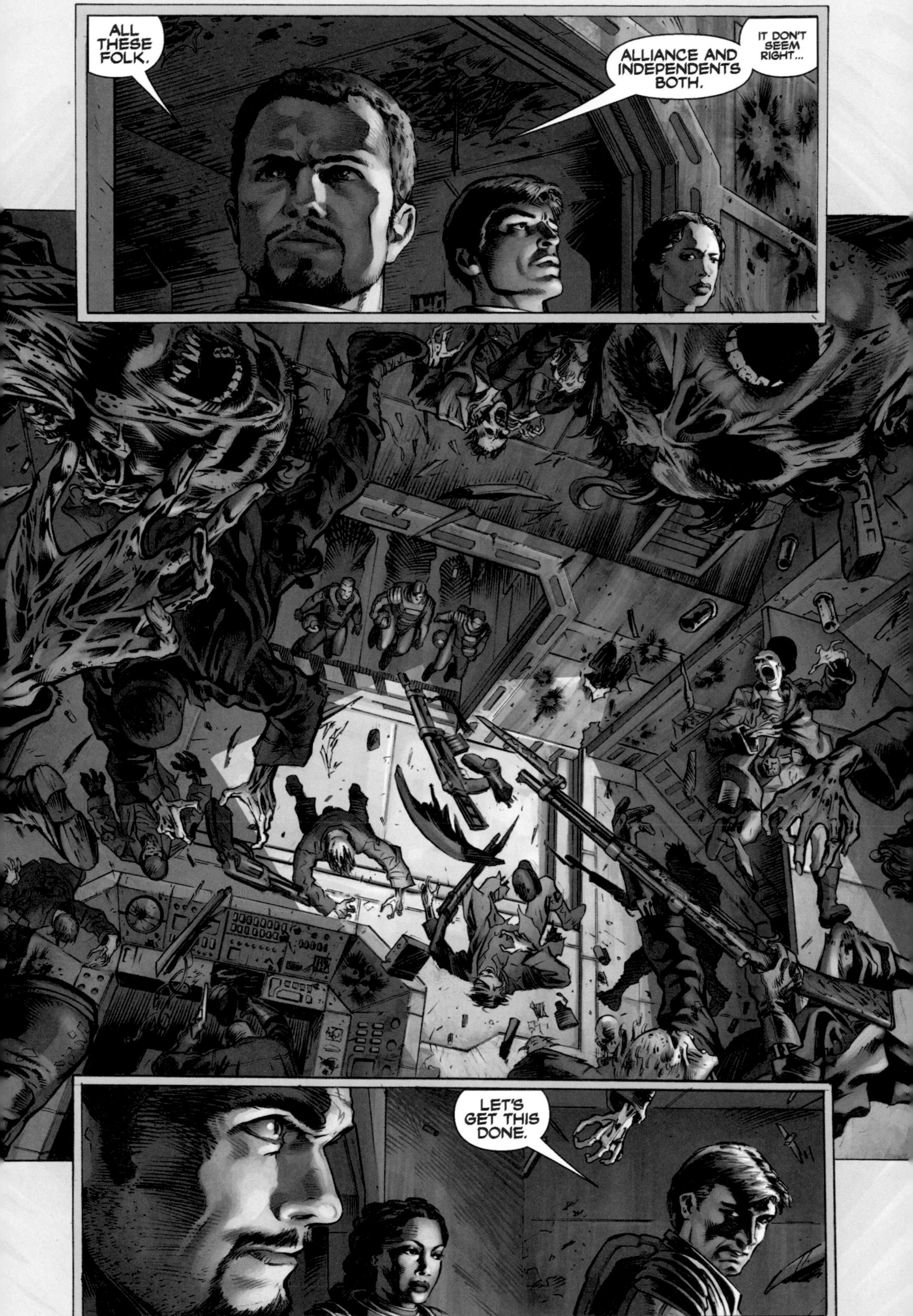
ALL THESE FOLK.
ALLIANCE AND INDEPENDENTS BOTH.
IT DON'T SEEM RIGHT...
LET'S GET THIS DONE.

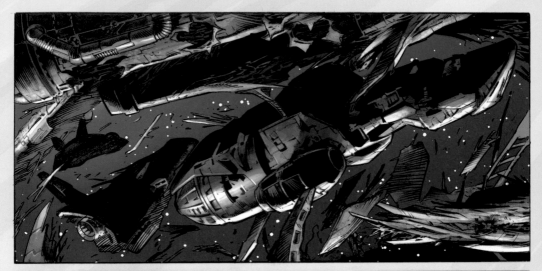

AIRLOCK ESTABLISHED.

PREPARE TO *BREACH.*

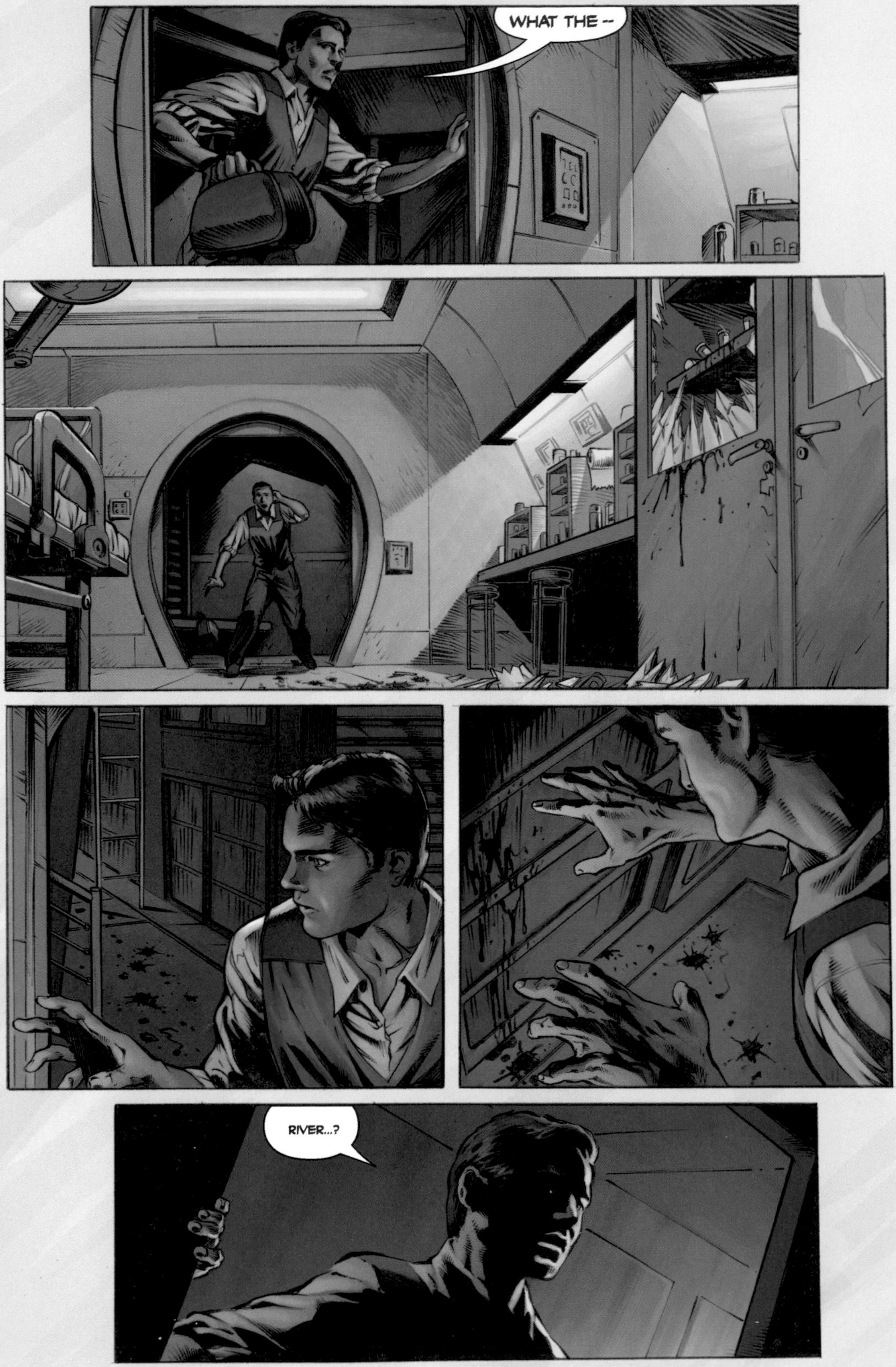
WHAT THE --
RIVER...?

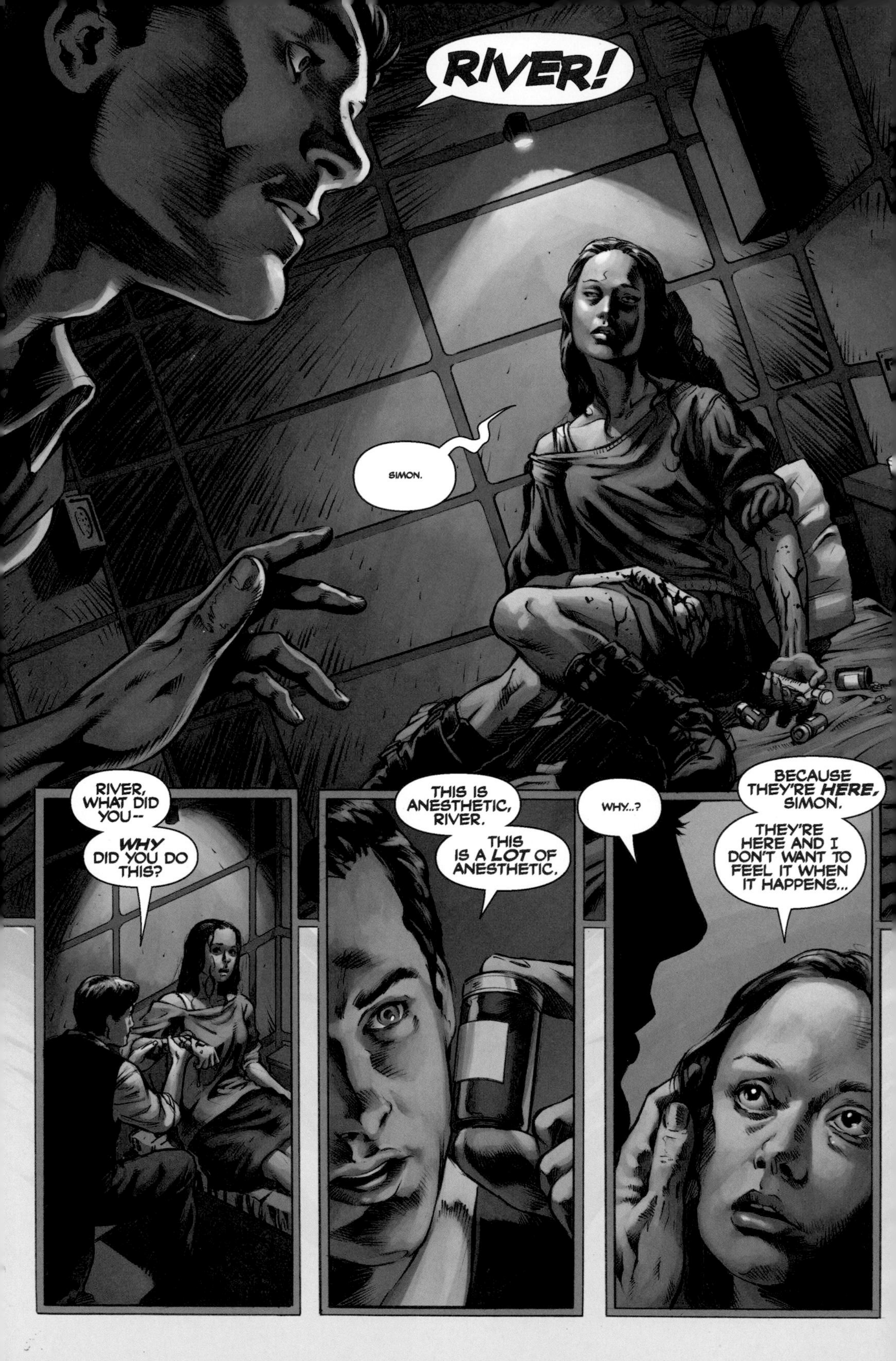
RIVER!
SIMON.
RIVER, WHAT DID YOU--
WHY DID YOU DO THIS?
THIS IS ANESTHETIC, RIVER.
THIS IS A LOT OF ANESTHETIC.
WHY...?
BECAUSE THEY'RE HERE, SIMON.
THEY'RE HERE AND I DON'T WANT TO FEEL IT WHEN IT HAPPENS...

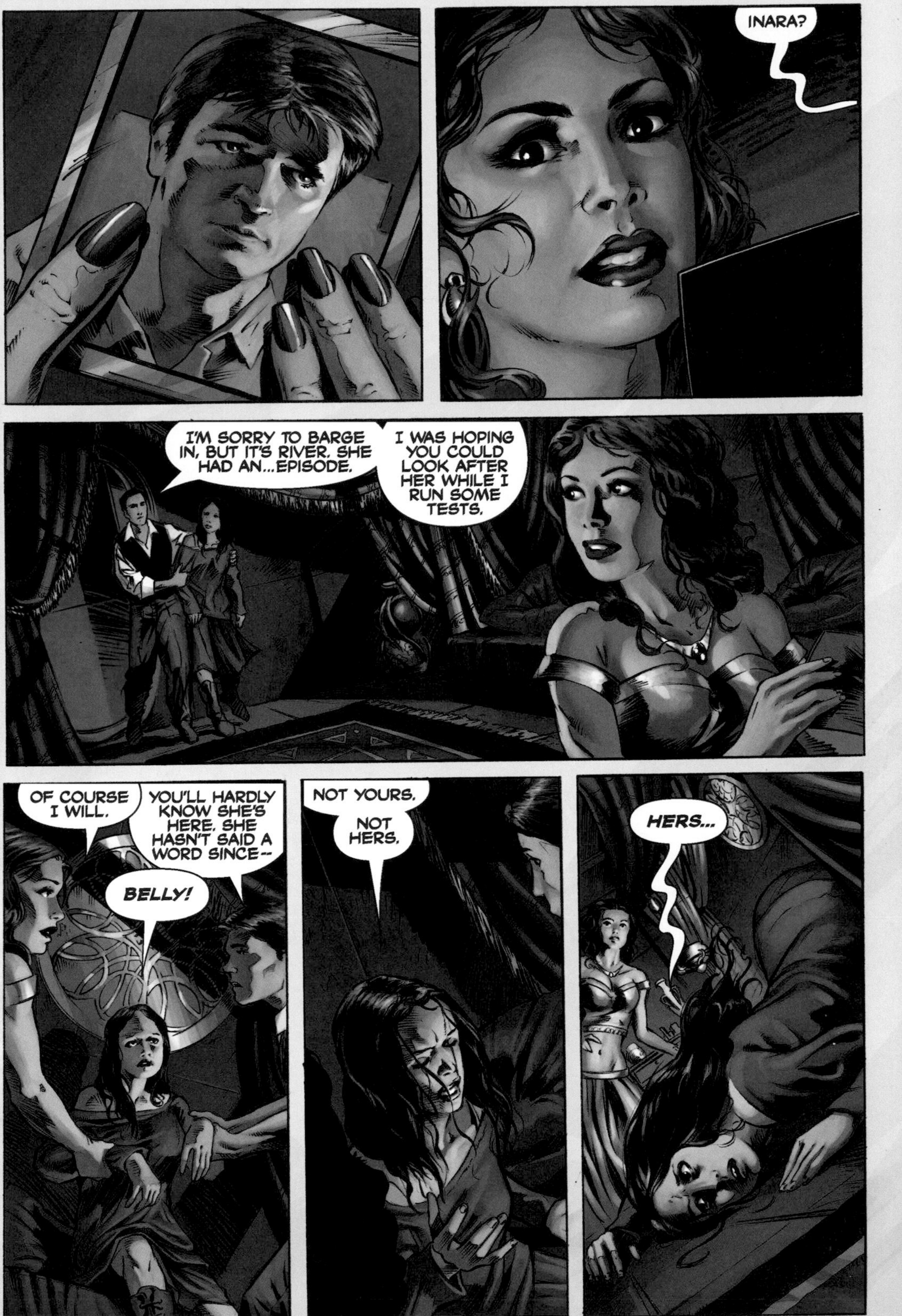
INARA?
I'M SORRY TO BARGE IN, BUT IT'S RIVER. SHE HAD AN...EPISODE.
I WAS HOPING YOU COULD LOOK AFTER HER WHILE I RUN SOME TESTS.
OF COURSE I WILL.
YOU'LL HARDLY KNOW SHE'S HERE. SHE HASN'T SAID A WORD SINCE--
BELLY!
NOT YOURS.
NOT HERS.
HERS...

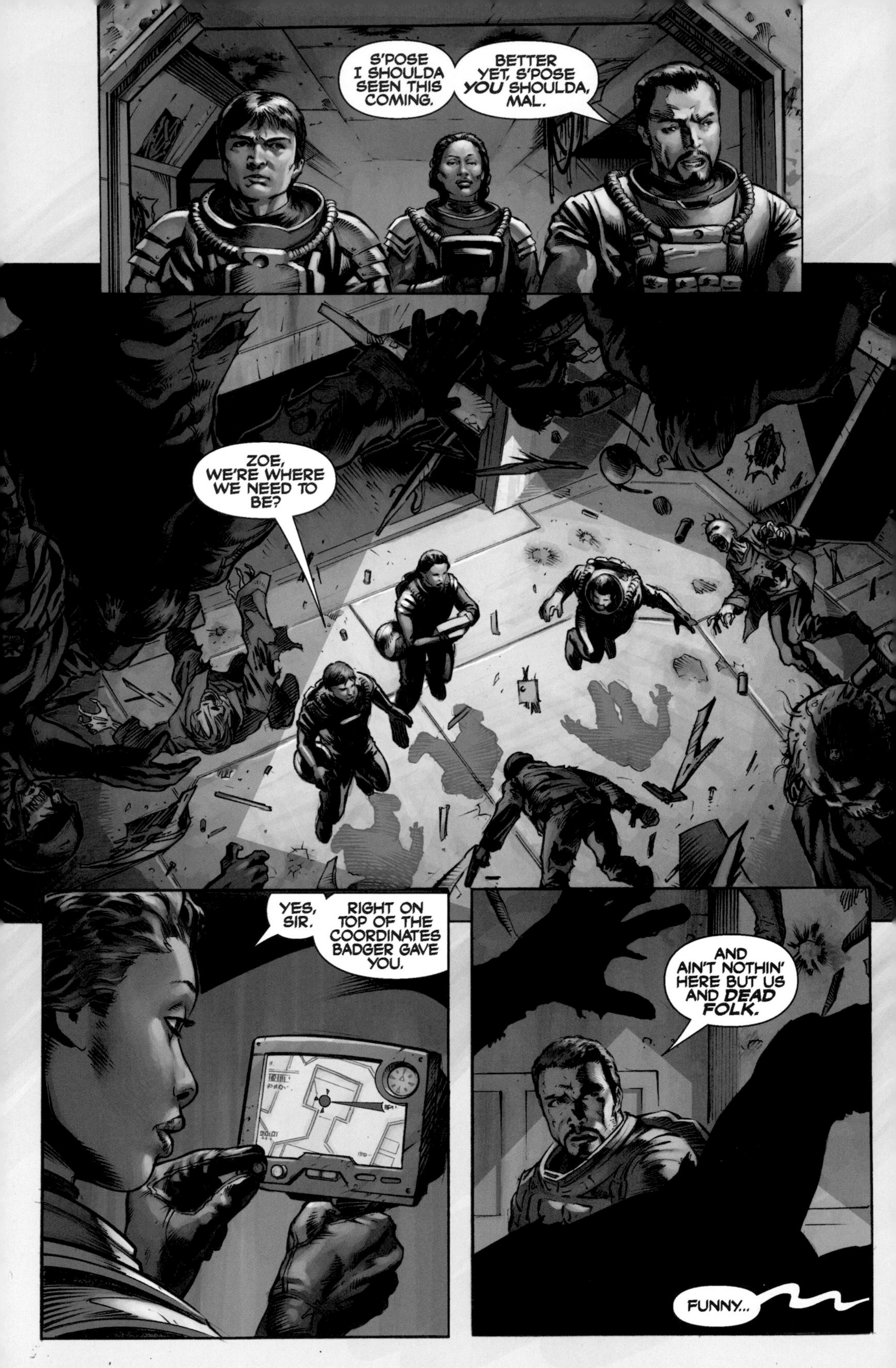
S'POSE I SHOULDA SEEN THIS COMING.
BETTER YET, S'POSE *YOU* SHOULDA, MAL.
ZOE, WE'RE WHERE WE NEED TO BE?
YES, SIR.
RIGHT ON TOP OF THE COORDINATES BADGER GAVE YOU.
AND AIN'T NOTHIN' HERE BUT US AND ***DEAD FOLK.***
FUNNY...

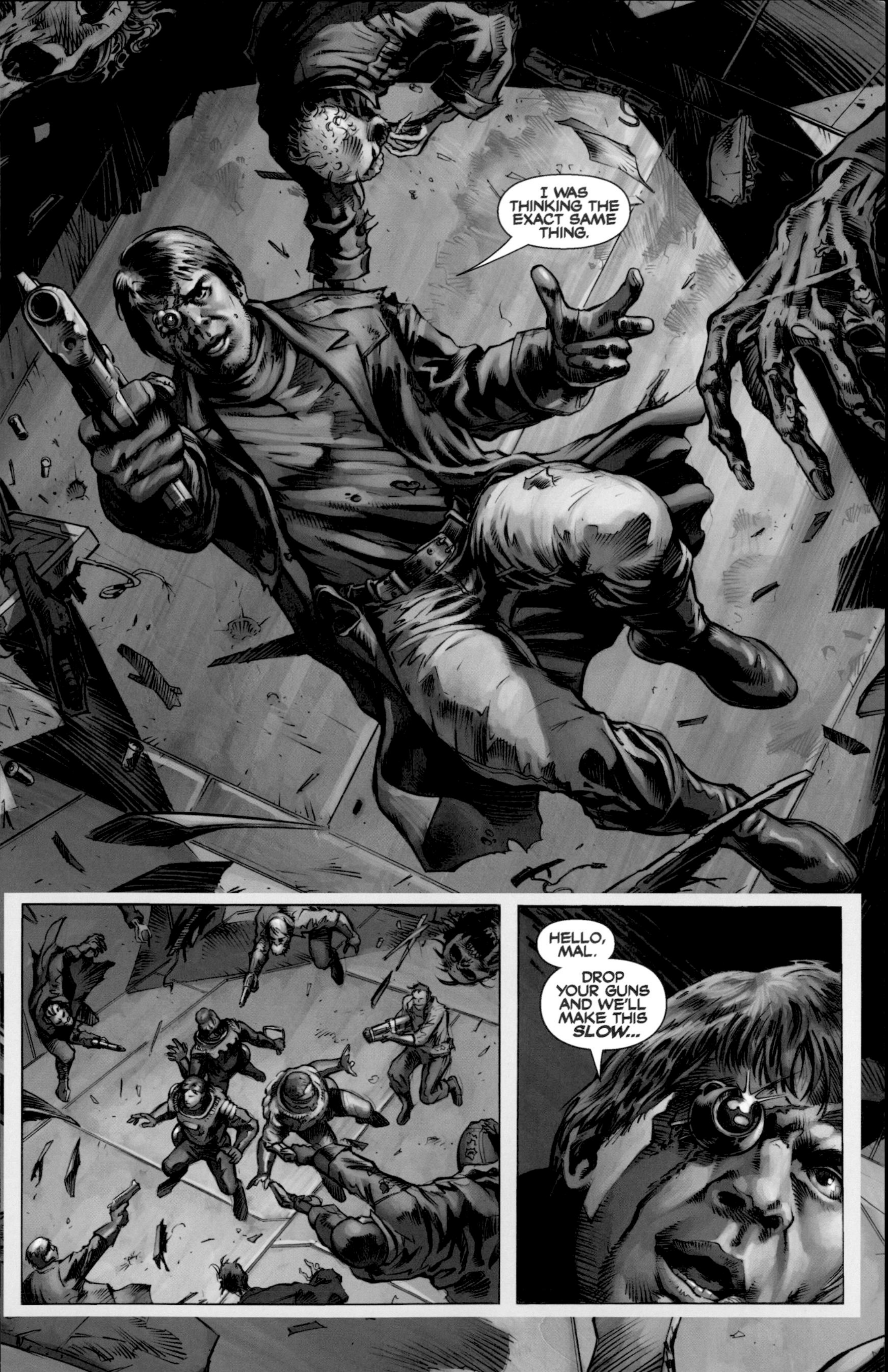
I WAS THINKING THE EXACT SAME THING.
HELLO, MAL.
DROP YOUR GUNS AND WE'LL MAKE THIS *SLOW...*

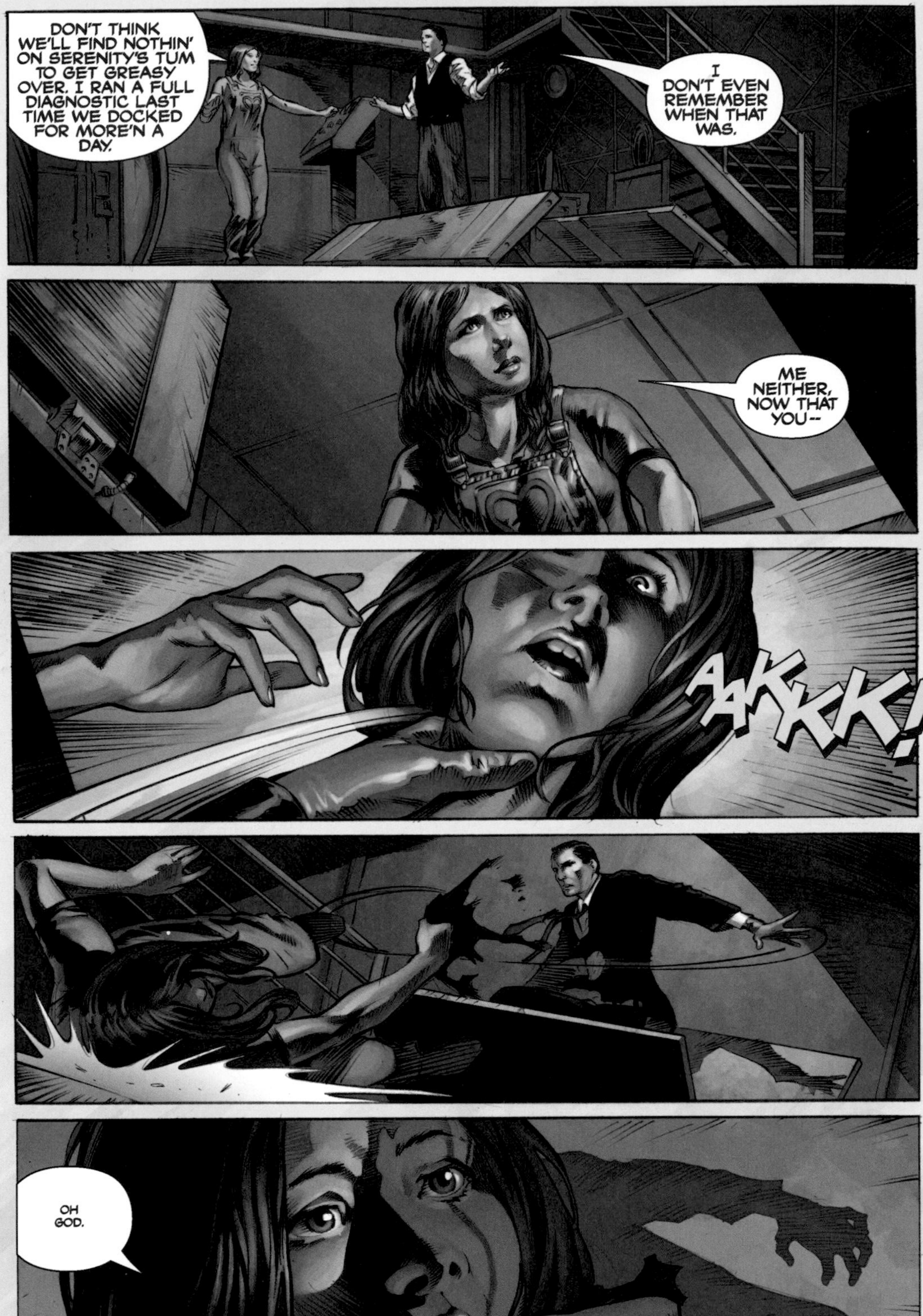
DON'T THINK WE'LL FIND NOTHIN' ON SERENITY'S TUM TO GET GREASY OVER. I RAN A FULL DIAGNOSTIC LAST TIME WE DOCKED FOR MORE'N A DAY.
I DON'T EVEN REMEMBER WHEN THAT WAS.
ME NEITHER, NOW THAT YOU--
AAKKK!
OH GOD.

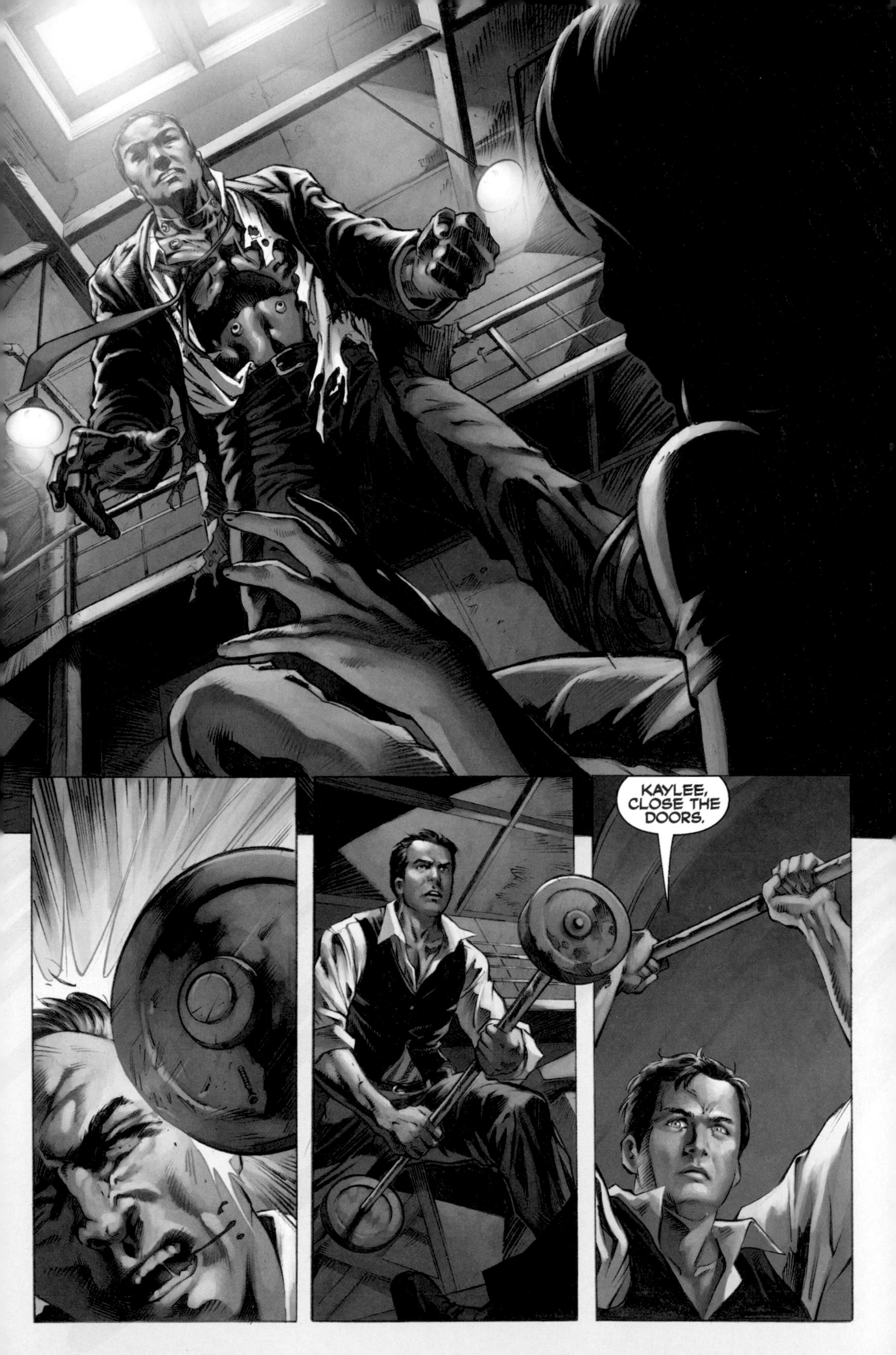
KAYLEE, CLOSE THE DOORS.

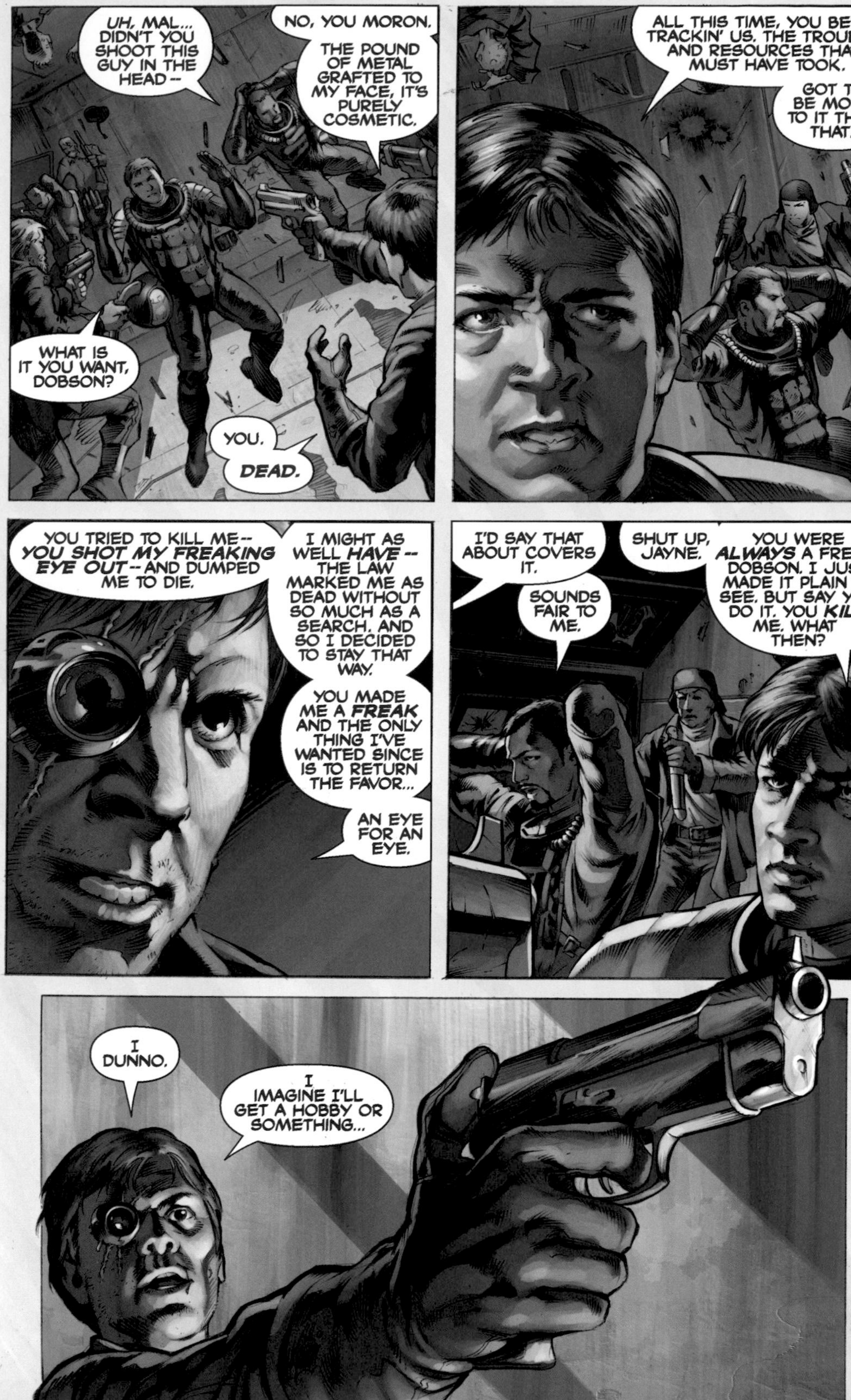
UH, MAL... DIDN'T YOU SHOOT THIS GUY IN THE HEAD --
NO, YOU MORON.
THE POUND OF METAL GRAFTED TO MY FACE, IT'S PURELY COSMETIC.
WHAT IS IT YOU WANT, DOBSON?
YOU.
DEAD.
ALL THIS TIME, YOU BEEN TRACKIN' US. THE TROUBLE AND RESOURCES THAT MUST HAVE TOOK.
GOT TO BE MORE TO IT THAN THAT...
YOU TRIED TO KILL ME -- YOU SHOT MY FREAKING EYE OUT -- AND DUMPED ME TO DIE.
I MIGHT AS WELL HAVE -- THE LAW MARKED ME AS DEAD WITHOUT SO MUCH AS A SEARCH. AND SO I DECIDED TO STAY THAT WAY.
YOU MADE ME A FREAK AND THE ONLY THING I'VE WANTED SINCE IS TO RETURN THE FAVOR...
AN EYE FOR AN EYE.
I'D SAY THAT ABOUT COVERS IT.
SOUNDS FAIR TO ME.
SHUT UP, JAYNE.
YOU WERE ALWAYS A FREAK, DOBSON. I JUST MADE IT PLAIN TO SEE. BUT SAY YOU DO IT. YOU KILL ME. WHAT THEN?
I DUNNO.
I IMAGINE I'LL GET A HOBBY OR SOMETHING...

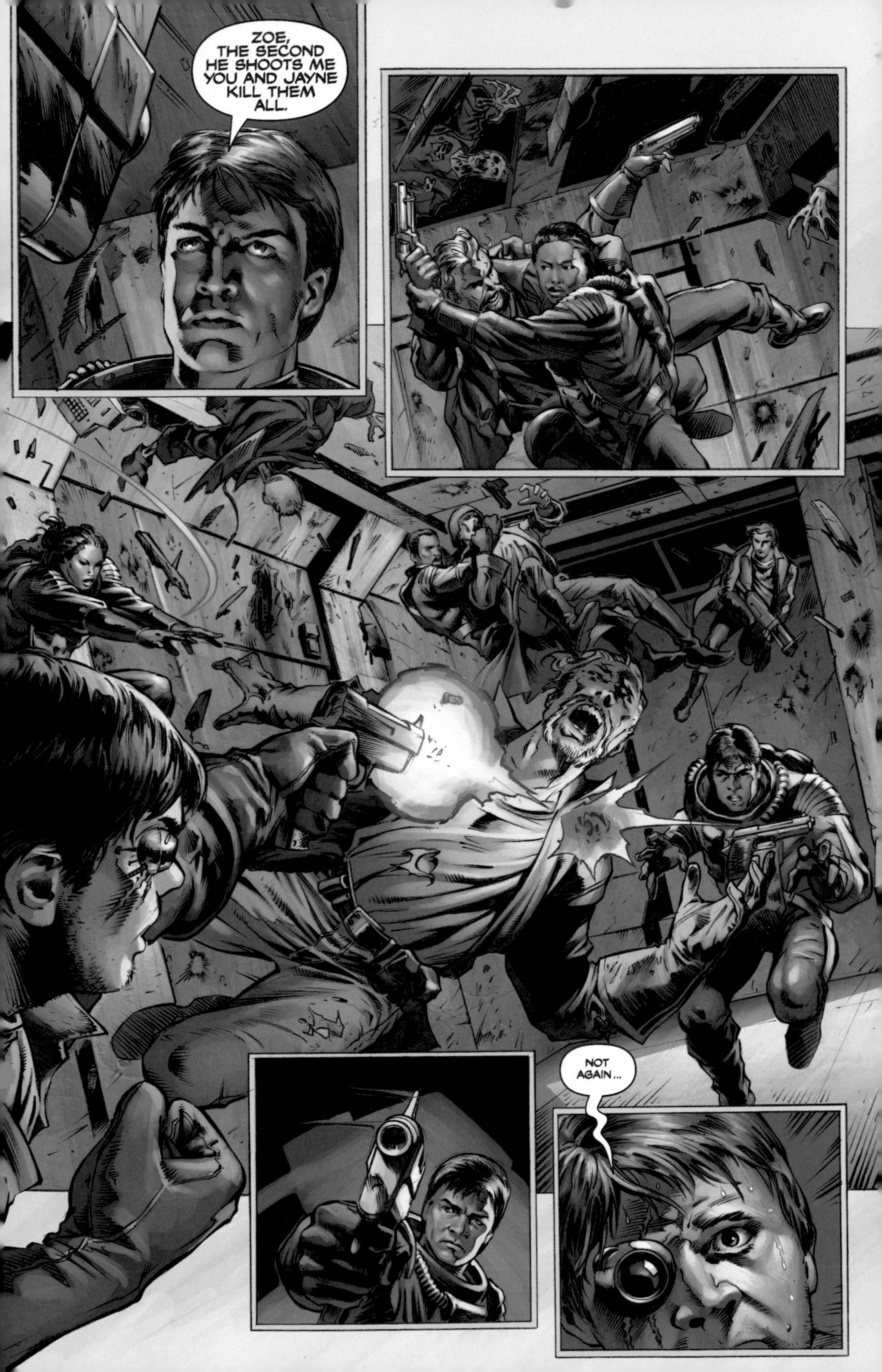
ZOE, THE SECOND HE SHOOTS ME YOU AND JAYNE KILL THEM ALL.
NOT AGAIN...

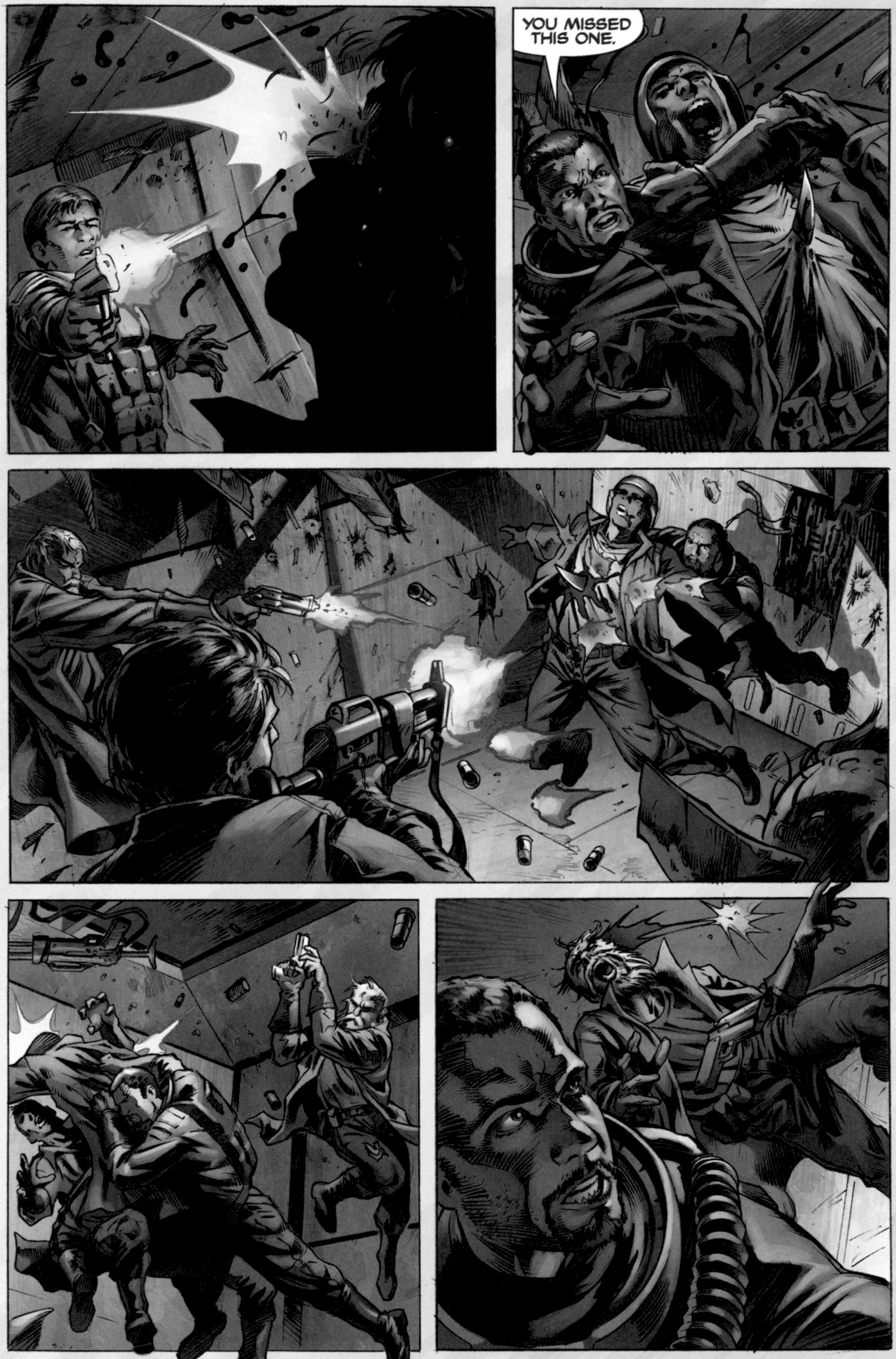
YOU MISSED THIS ONE.

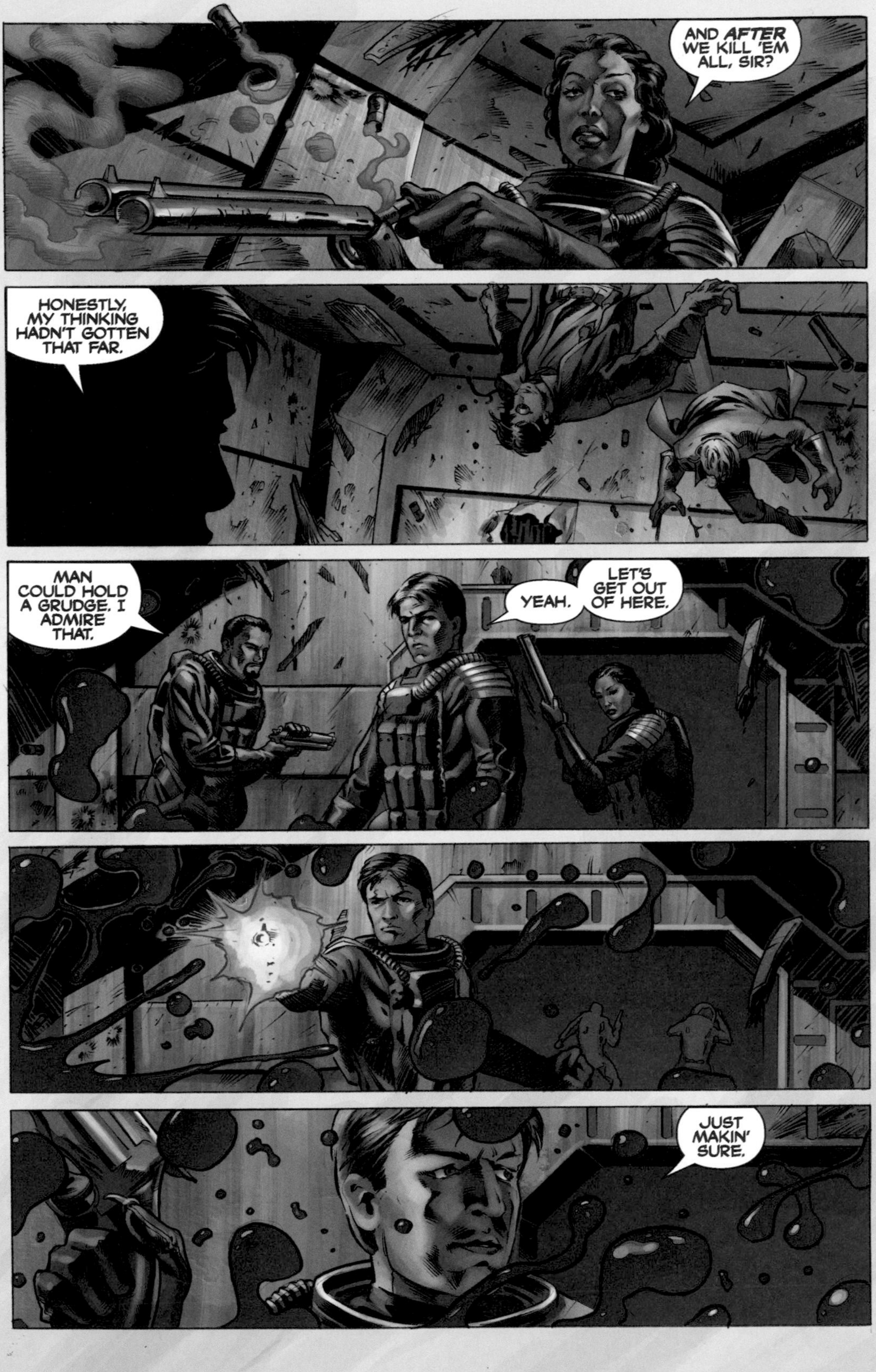
AND AFTER WE KILL 'EM ALL, SIR?
HONESTLY, MY THINKING HADN'T GOTTEN THAT FAR.
MAN COULD HOLD A GRUDGE. I ADMIRE THAT.
YEAH.
LET'S GET OUT OF HERE.
JUST MAKIN' SURE.

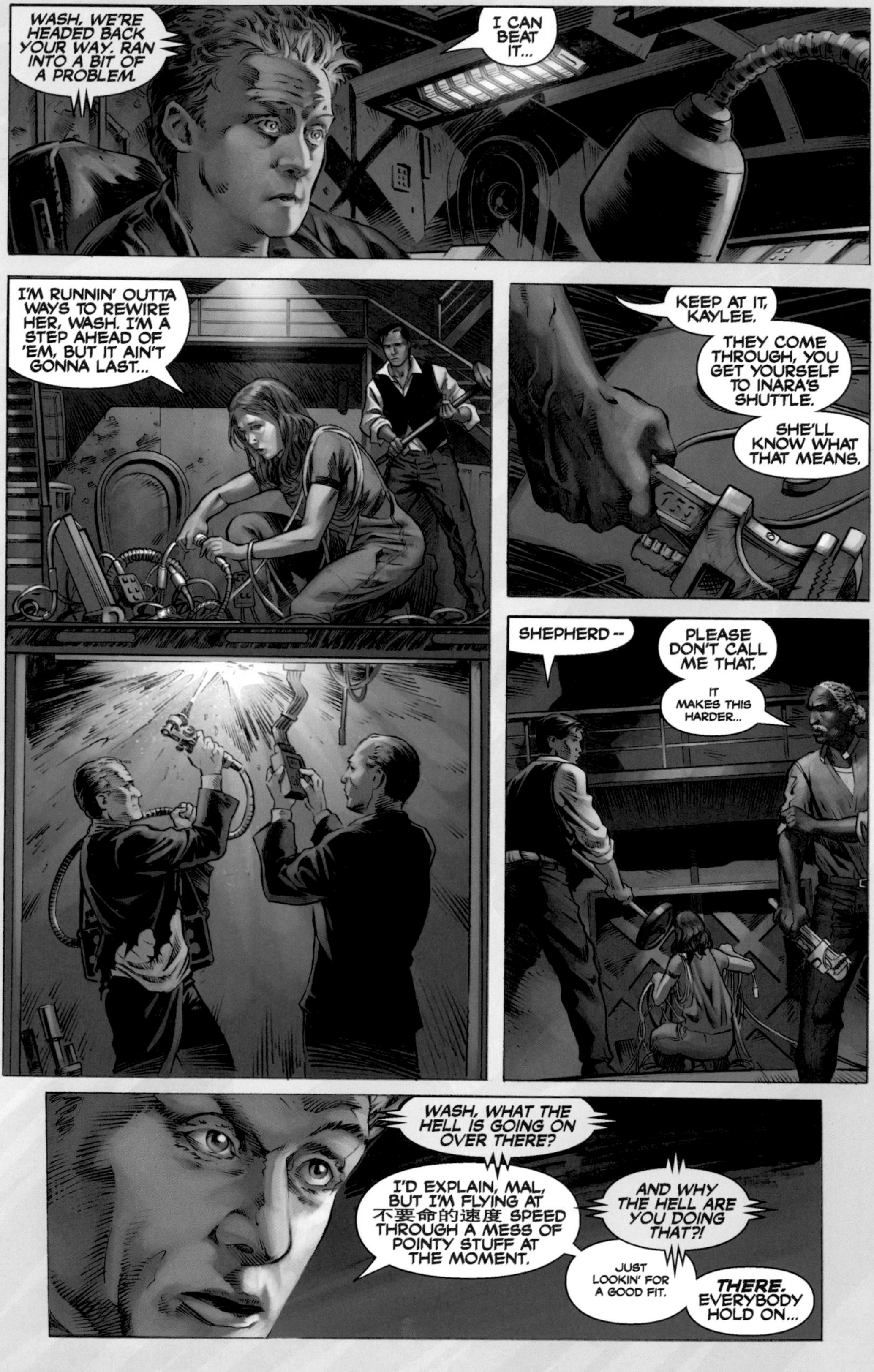
WASH, WE'RE HEADED BACK YOUR WAY. RAN INTO A BIT OF A PROBLEM.
I CAN BEAT IT...
I'M RUNNIN' OUTTA WAYS TO REWIRE HER, WASH. I'M A STEP AHEAD OF 'EM, BUT IT AIN'T GONNA LAST...
KEEP AT IT, KAYLEE.
THEY COME THROUGH, YOU GET YOURSELF TO INARA'S SHUTTLE.
SHE'LL KNOW WHAT THAT MEANS.
SHEPHERD --
PLEASE DON'T CALL ME THAT.
IT MAKES THIS HARDER...
WASH, WHAT THE HELL IS GOING ON OVER THERE?
I'D EXPLAIN, MAL, BUT I'M FLYING AT 不要命的速度 SPEED THROUGH A MESS OF POINTY STUFF AT THE MOMENT.
AND WHY THE HELL ARE YOU DOING THAT?!
JUST LOOKIN' FOR A GOOD FIT.
THERE. EVERYBODY HOLD ON...

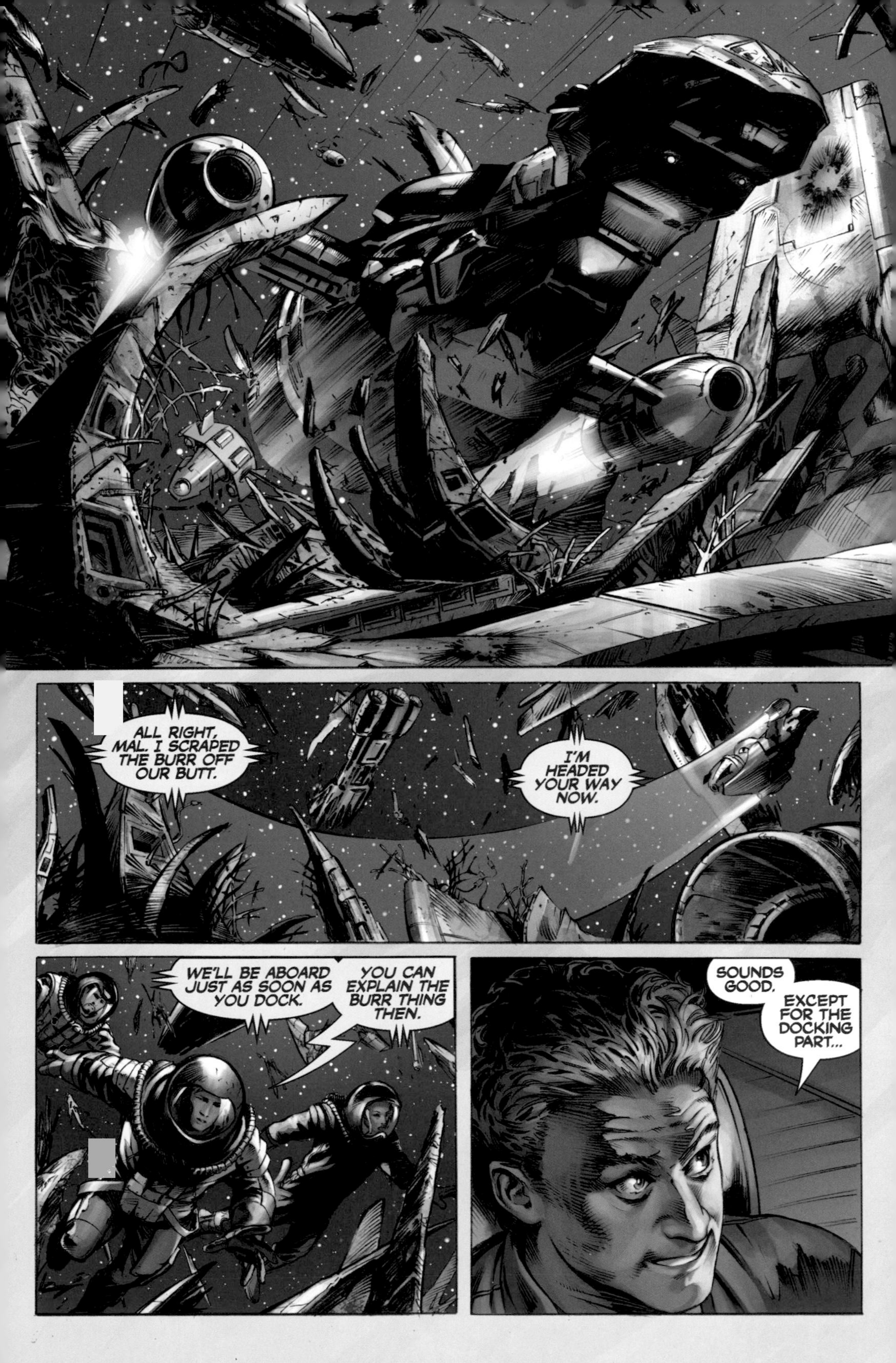
ALL RIGHT, MAL. I SCRAPED THE BURR OFF OUR BUTT.
I'M HEADED YOUR WAY NOW.
WE'LL BE ABOARD JUST AS SOON AS YOU DOCK.
YOU CAN EXPLAIN THE BURR THING THEN.
SOUNDS GOOD,
EXCEPT FOR THE DOCKING PART...

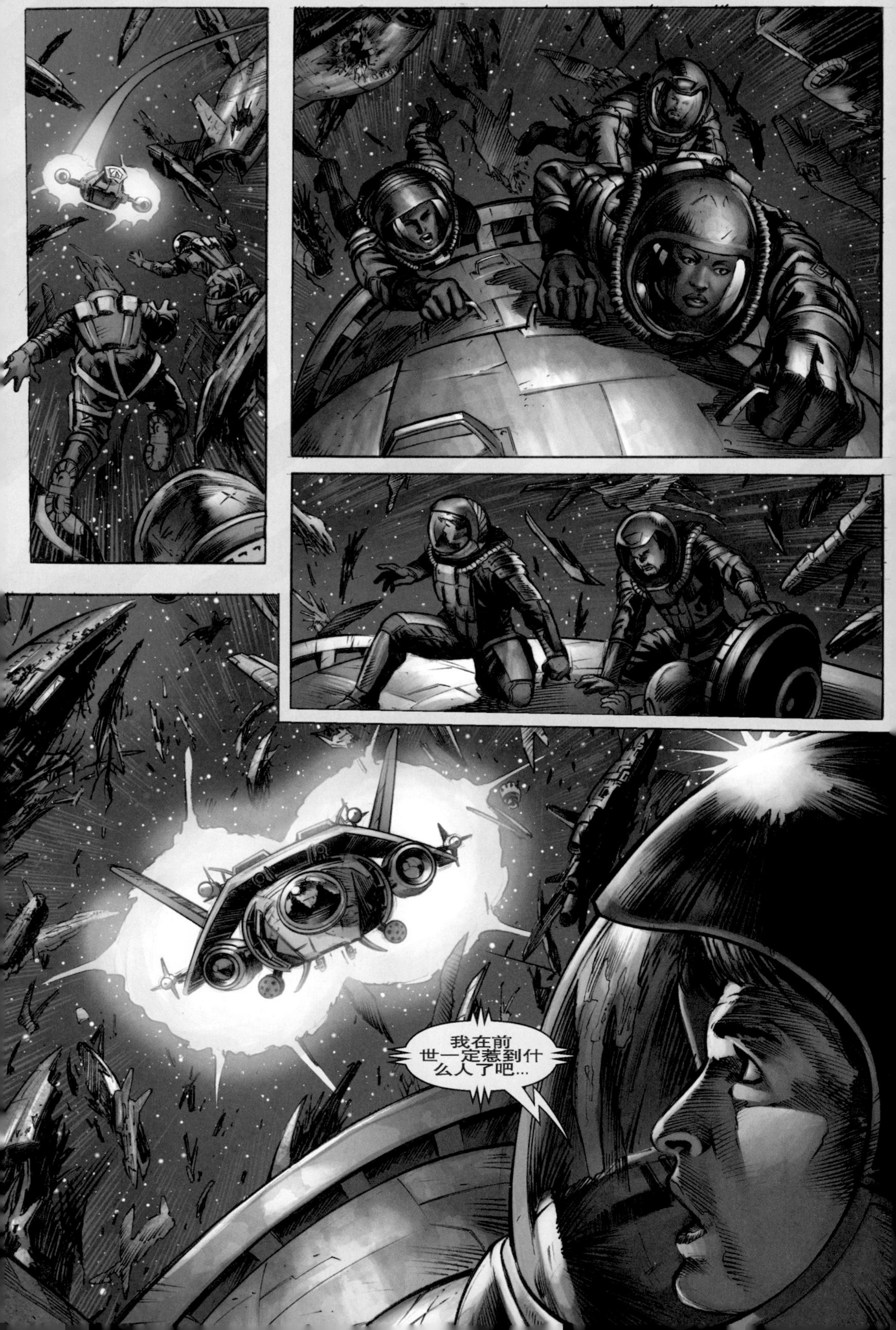
我在前
世一定惹到什
么人了吧...

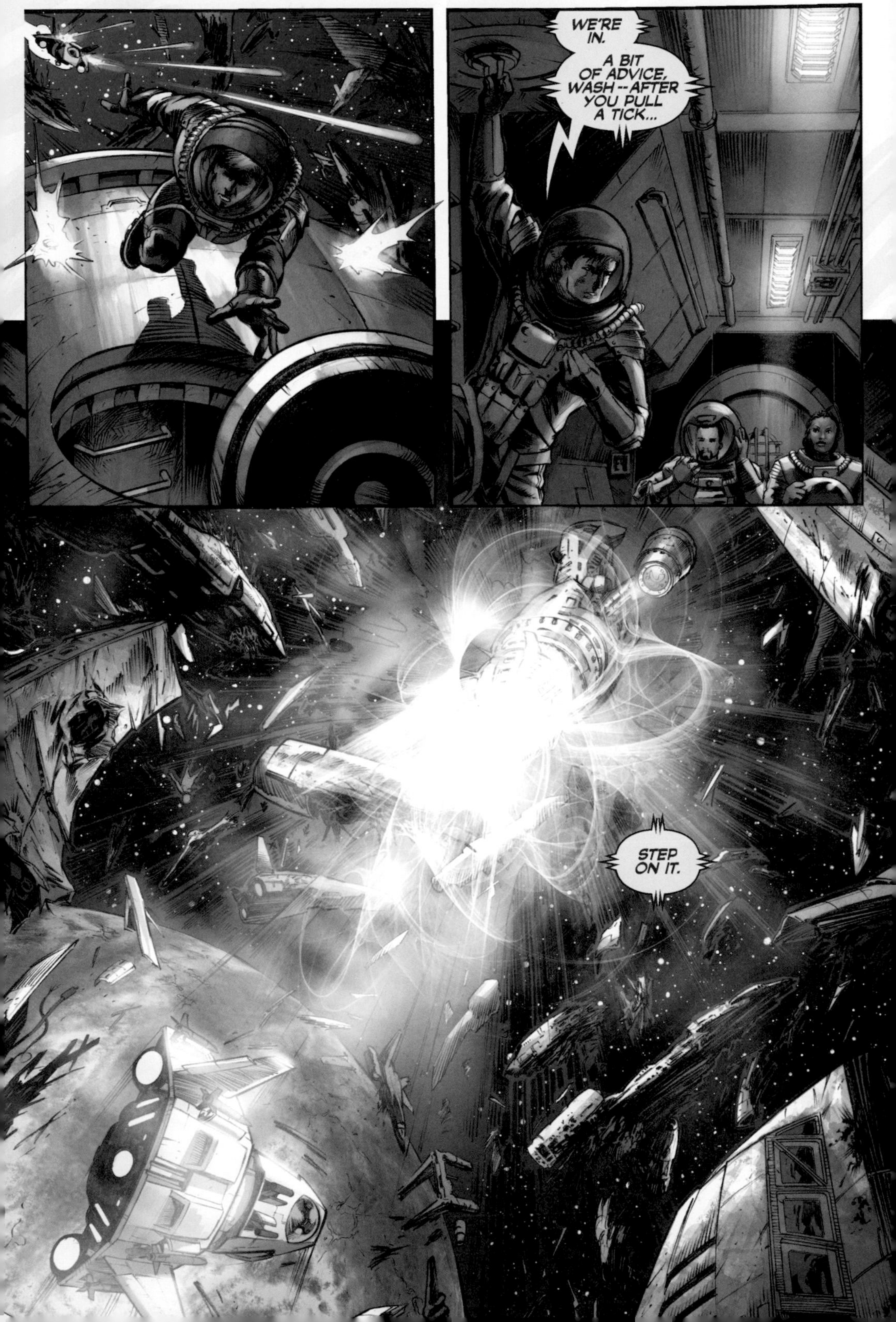
WE'RE IN.
A BIT OF ADVICE, WASH --AFTER YOU PULL A TICK...
STEP ON IT.

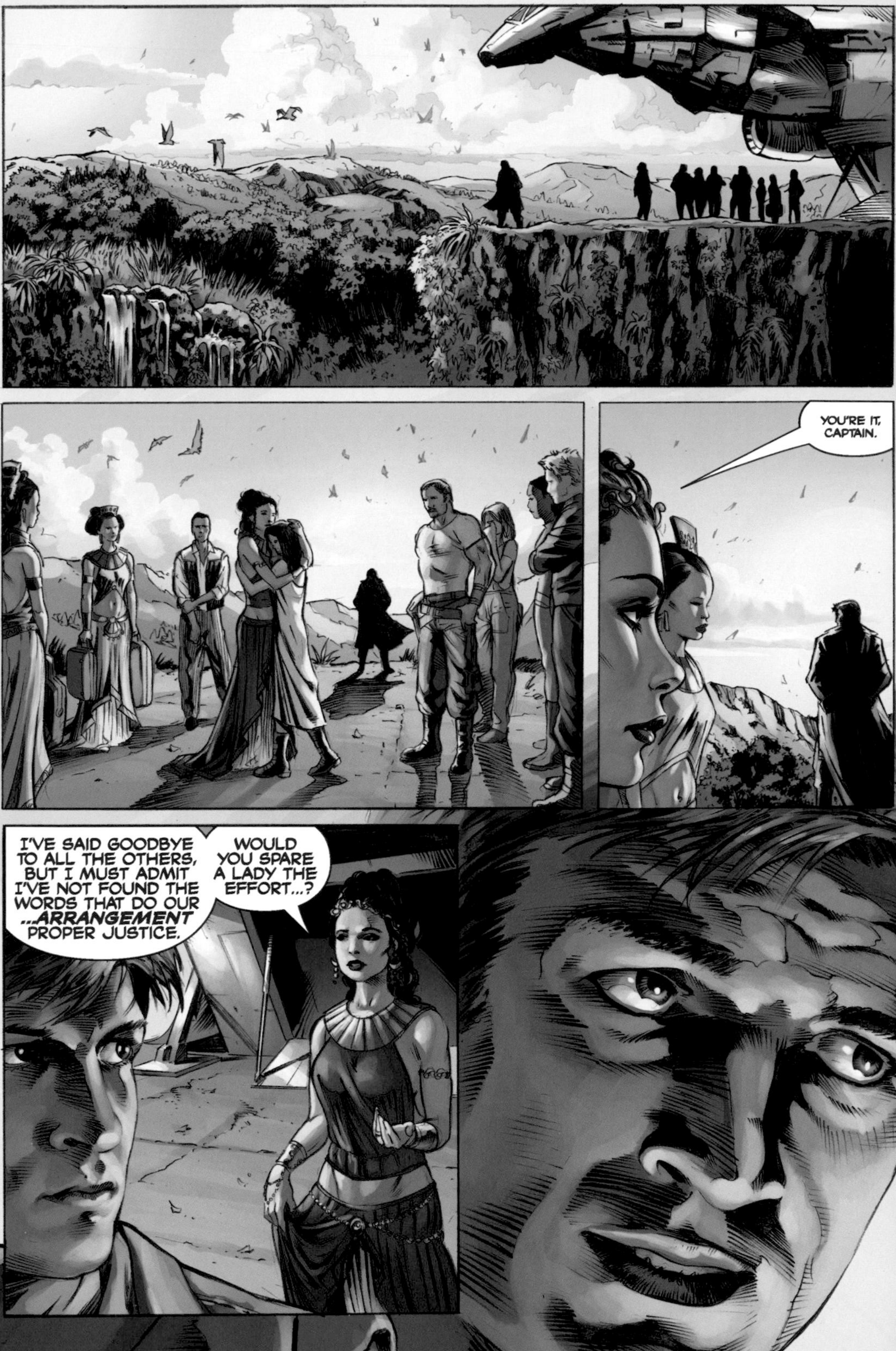
YOU'RE IT, CAPTAIN.
I'VE SAID GOODBYE TO ALL THE OTHERS, BUT I MUST ADMIT I'VE NOT FOUND THE WORDS THAT DO OUR ...ARRANGEMENT PROPER JUSTICE.
WOULD YOU SPARE A LADY THE EFFORT...?

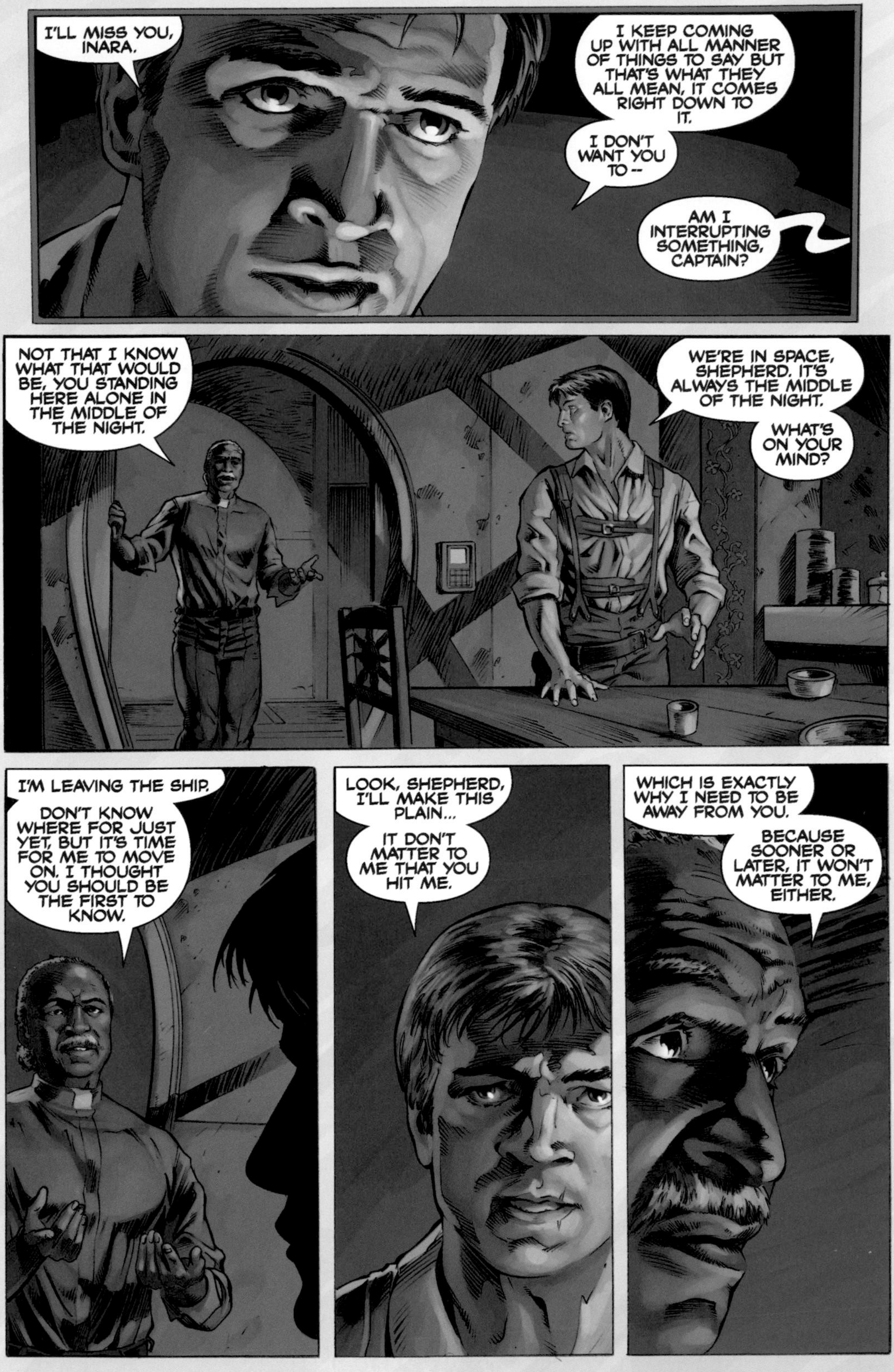
I'LL MISS YOU, INARA.
I KEEP COMING UP WITH ALL MANNER OF THINGS TO SAY BUT THAT'S WHAT THEY ALL MEAN, IT COMES RIGHT DOWN TO IT.
I DON'T WANT YOU TO --
AM I INTERRUPTING SOMETHING, CAPTAIN?
NOT THAT I KNOW WHAT THAT WOULD BE, YOU STANDING HERE ALONE IN THE MIDDLE OF THE NIGHT.
WE'RE IN SPACE, SHEPHERD. IT'S ALWAYS THE MIDDLE OF THE NIGHT.
WHAT'S ON YOUR MIND?
I'M LEAVING THE SHIP.
DON'T KNOW WHERE FOR JUST YET, BUT IT'S TIME FOR ME TO MOVE ON. I THOUGHT YOU SHOULD BE THE FIRST TO KNOW.
LOOK, SHEPHERD, I'LL MAKE THIS PLAIN...
IT DON'T MATTER TO ME THAT YOU HIT ME.
WHICH IS EXACTLY WHY I NEED TO BE AWAY FROM YOU.
BECAUSE SOONER OR LATER, IT WON'T MATTER TO ME, EITHER.

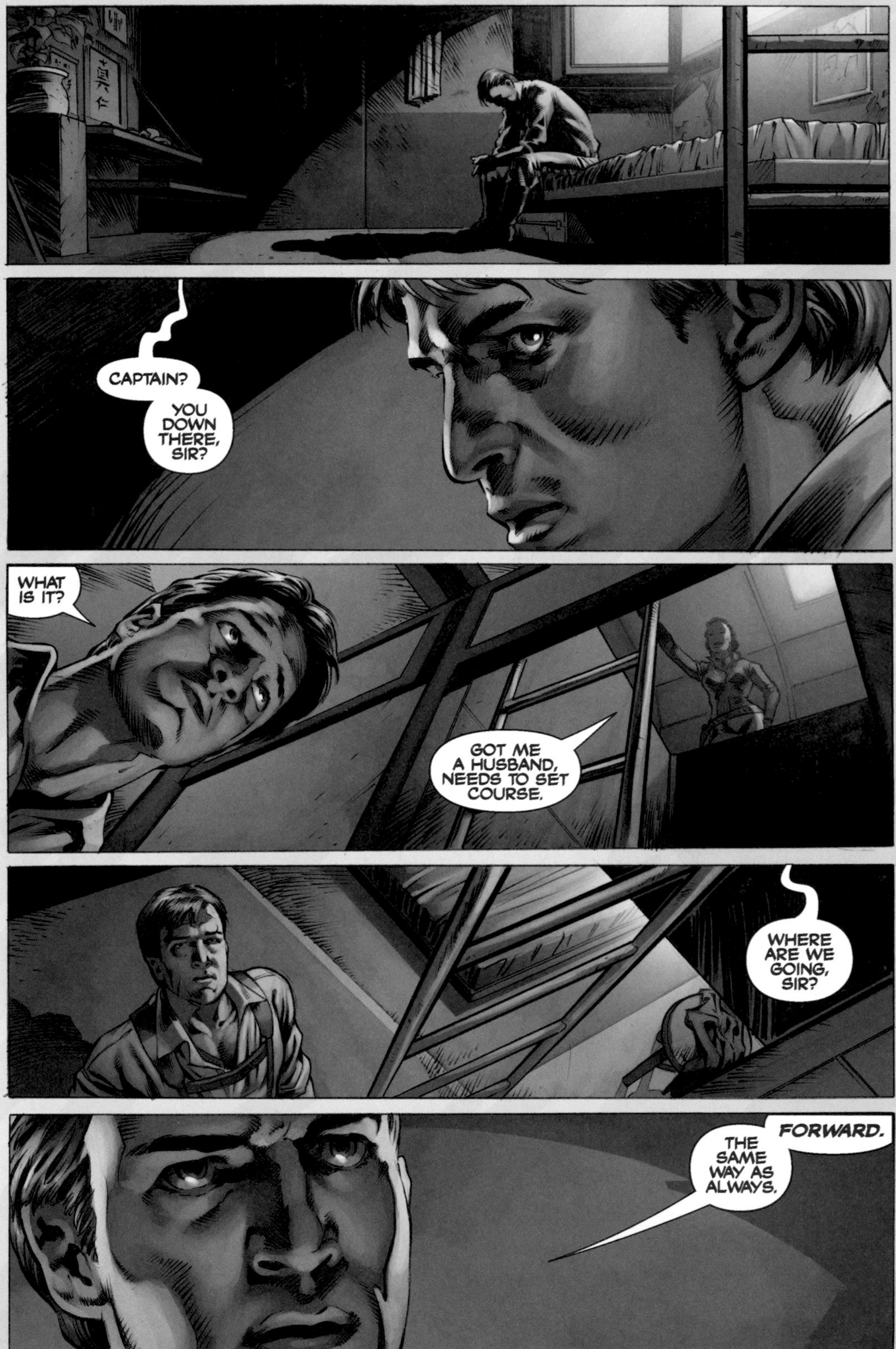
CAPTAIN?
YOU DOWN THERE, SIR?
WHAT IS IT?
GOT ME A HUSBAND, NEEDS TO SET COURSE.
WHERE ARE WE GOING, SIR?
FORWARD.
THE SAME WAY AS ALWAYS.

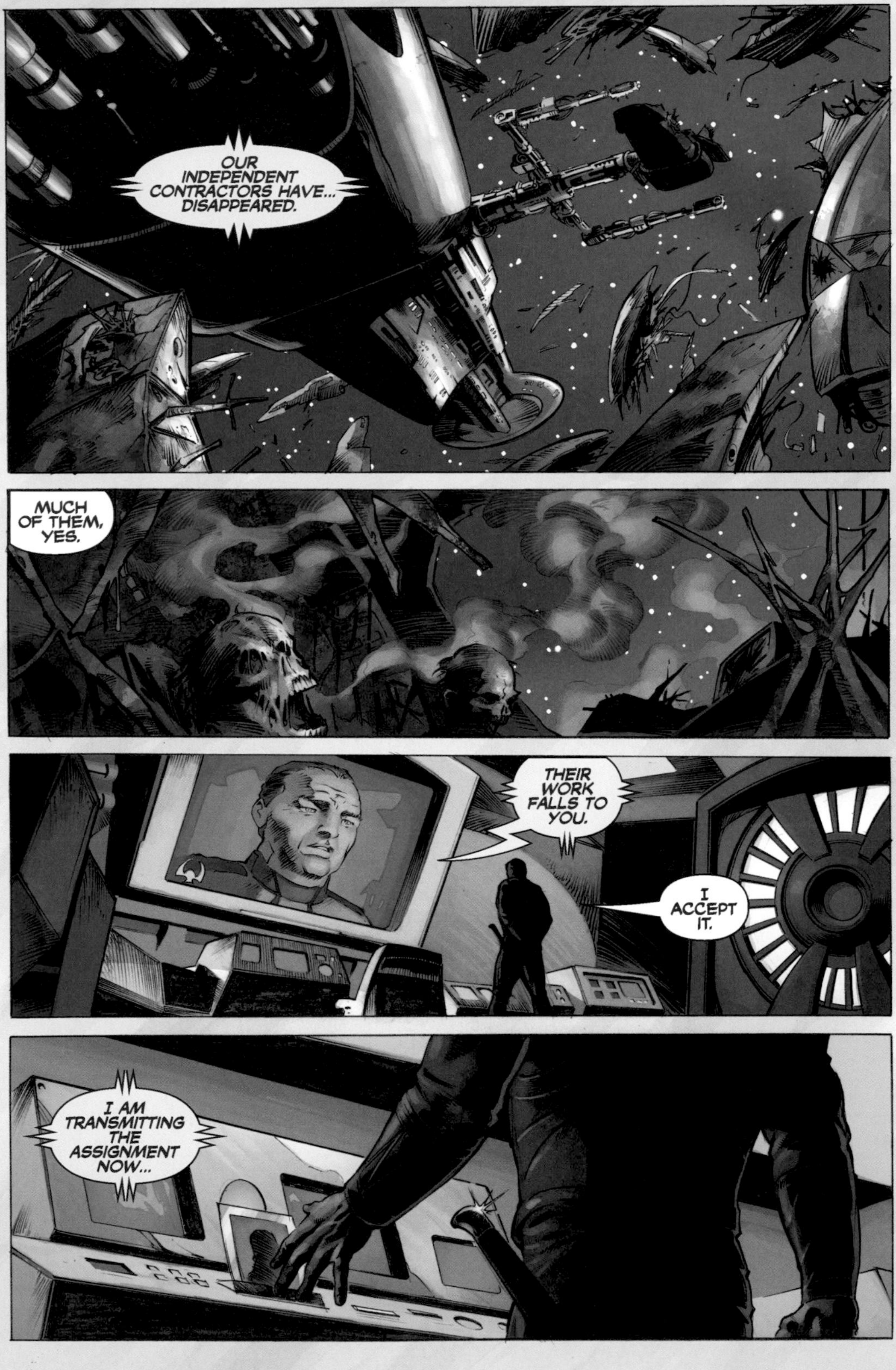
OUR INDEPENDENT CONTRACTORS HAVE... DISAPPEARED.
MUCH OF THEM, YES.
THEIR WORK FALLS TO YOU.
I ACCEPT IT.
I AM TRANSMITTING THE ASSIGNMENT NOW...

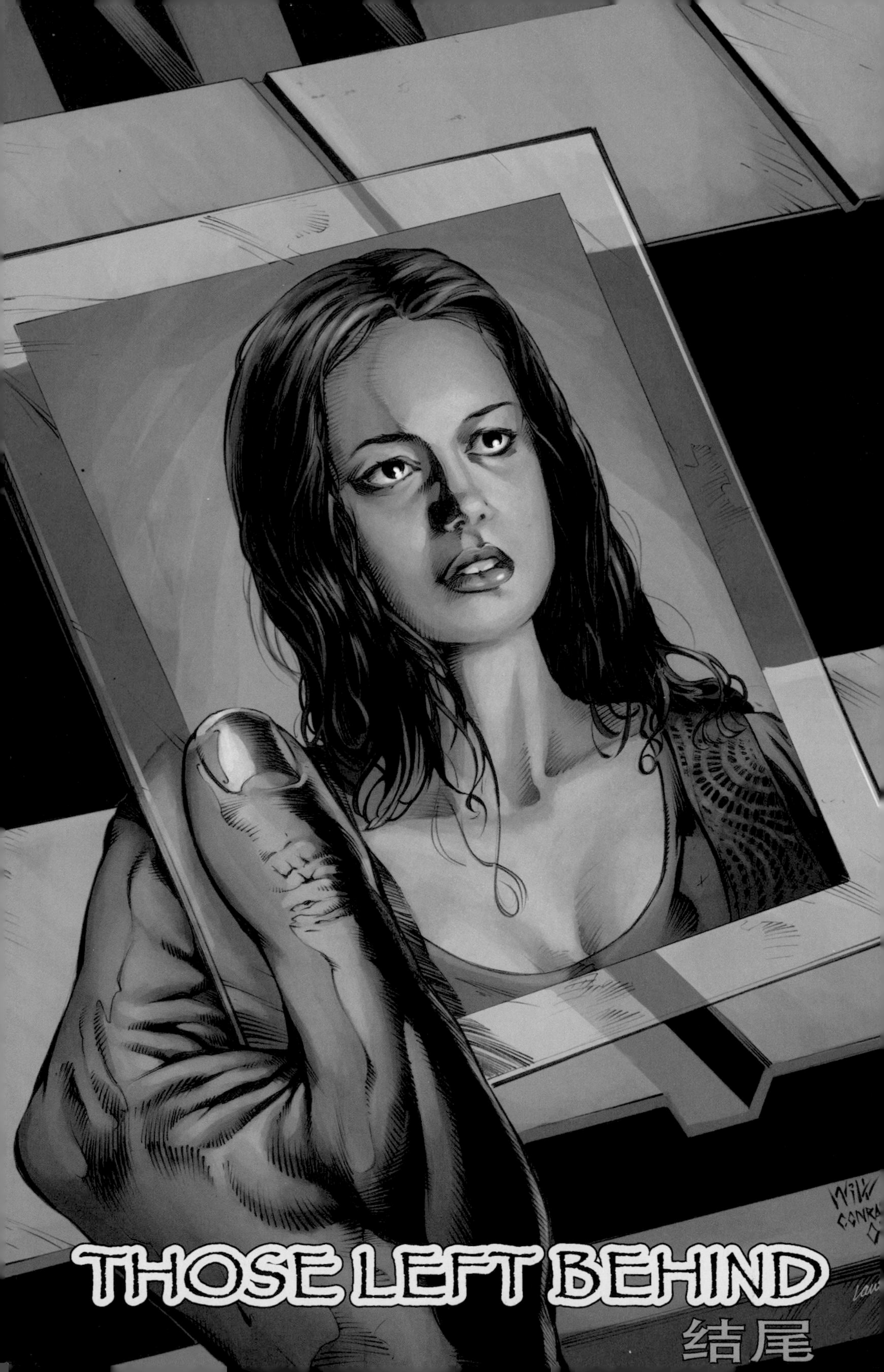
THOSE LEFT BEHIND
结尾

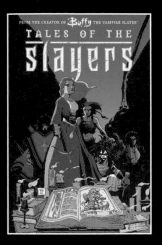

ALSO FROM JOSS WHEDON!

FROM THE CREATOR OF Buffy THE VAMPIRE SLAYER
TALES OF THE
slayers

BUFFY THE VAMPIRE SLAYER: TALES OF THE SLAYERS

Joss Whedon, Leinil Francis Yu, Tim Sale, Brett Matthews, and others

Buffy Summers is only the latest in a long line of young women who have battled vampires, demons, and other forces of evil as the Slayer. Now, hear the stories behind other Slayers, past and future, told by the writers of the hit television show and illustrated by some of the most acclaimed artists in comics.

ISBN: 1-56971-605-6 $14.95

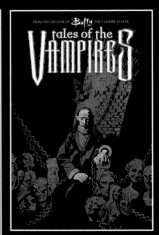

FROM THE CREATOR OF Buffy THE VAMPIRE SLAYER
tales of the
VAMPIRES

BUFFY THE VAMPIRE SLAYER: TALES OF THE VAMPIRES

Joss Whedon, Brett Matthews, Cameron Stewart, Tim Sale, and others

The creator of *Buffy the Vampire Slayer* and *Angel* reunites with the writers from his hit TV shows for a frightening look into the history of vampires. Illustrated by some of comics' greatest artists, the stories span medieval times to today, including Buffy's rematch with Dracula, and Angel's ongoing battle with his own demons.

ISBN: 1-56971-749-4 $15.95

joss whedon
karl moline
andy owens
FRAY

FRAY

Joss Whedon, Karl Moline, and Andy Owens

In a future Manhattan so poisoned it doesn't notice the monsters on its streets, it's up to a gutter punk named Fray to unite a fallen city against a demonic plot to consume mankind. But will this girl who thought she had no future embrace her destiny—as the first Vampire Slayer in centuries—in time?

ISBN: 1-56971-751-6 $19.95

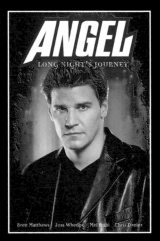

ANGEL
LONG NIGHT'S JOURNEY
Brett Matthews Joss Whedon Mel Rubi Chris Dreier

ANGEL: LONG NIGHT'S JOURNEY

Joss Whedon, Brett Matthews, and Mel Rubi

An enemy from Angel's past has come to L.A. Now, in one catastrophic night, Angel must go toe-to-toe with three of the most powerful monsters he has ever faced. Together, Brett Matthews and *Angel* creator Joss Whedon retool and reinvent Angel, crafting a story so big it wouldn't fit on the small screen.

ISBN: 1-56971-752-4 $12.95

ALSO FROM DARK HORSE BOOKS!

Scarlet Traces
Ian Edginton · D'Israeli

SCARLET TRACES

Ian Edginton and D'Israeli

A decade after the failed Martian invasion of England, the industrious Victorians have assimilated Martian technologies to assure British dominance over the Earth. However, something rotten at the heart of the Empire is revealed when bodies drained of blood start washing up on the Thames. A hardcover original graphic novel.

ISBN: 1-56971-940-3 $14.95

"Classic SF adventure, reminiscent of Heinlein at his best."
—Lawrence Watt-Evans
Kurt Busiek · Stuart Immonen · Wade Von Grawbadger
SHOCKROCKETS
WE HAVE IGNITION

SHOCK ROCKETS: WE HAVE IGNITION

Kurt Busiek, Stuart Immonen, and Wade Von Grawbadger

In the wake of a devastating alien war, Earth is protected by the Shockrockets—a squadron of aerial fighters built from a fusion of alien and human technology and piloted by the best Earth has to offer. Now they face a deadly challenge as the military genius who saved the planet makes an all-out attempt at global domination.

ISBN: 1-59307-129-9 $14.95

STAR WARS
EMPIRE
VOLUME ONE
BETRAYAL

STAR WARS: EMPIRE VOLUME 1: BETRAYAL

Scott Allie, Ryan Benjamin

In the weeks before the events in *Star Wars: A New Hope*, as the Death Star is readied for its fateful first mission, a power-hungry cabal of Grand Moffs and Imperial Officers embark on a dangerous plan to kill Emperor Palpatine and Darth Vader and seize control of the Empire!

ISBN: 1-56971-964-0 $12.95

LONE WOLF 2100
SHADOWS ON SAPLINGS
MIKE KENNEDY
FRANCISCO RUIZ VELASCO

LONE WOLF 2100 VOLUME 1: SHADOWS ON SAPLINGS

Mike Kennedy, Francisco Ruiz Velasco

A corporation is hunting a young girl with a powerful secret and her only ally is the android accused of murdering her father. Plunge into a re-imagining of the legendary manga *Lone Wolf and Cub* where human and android struggle for life in the hostile landscape of a dystopian future.

ISBN: 1-56971-893-8 $12.95

DARK HORSE BOOKS

AVAILABLE AT YOUR LOCAL COMICS SHOP OR BOOKSTORE

To find a comics shop in your area, call 1-888-266-4226

For more information or to order direct visit darkhorse.com or call 1-800-862-0052 Mon.–Fri. 9 A.M. to 5 P.M. Pacific Time

*Prices and availability subject to change without notice

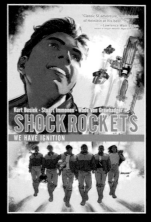

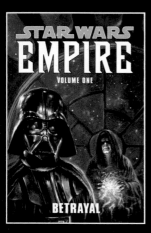

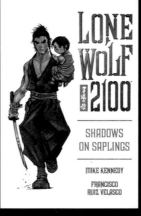